Behold Me, Behold Me
Evangelism That Glorifies God

S.M. Platt

Copyright © 2019 S.M. Platt

All rights reserved. No part of this publication may be reproduced by any means, graphic, electronic, or mechanical, including photocopying, recording, taping, or by any information storage retrieval system, without prior written permission of the author except in the case of brief quotations embodied in critical articles and reviews.

Because of the dynamic nature of the Internet, any web addresses or links contained in this book may have changed since publication and may no longer be valid.

All Scripture quotations from the
King James Version
of the Holy Bible.

ISBN: 9781794491717

DEDICATION

To my Lord and Savior, Jesus Christ. I pray that this book will be glorifying to God and instrumental in bringing many others to repentance and faith.

CONTENTS

    Dedication   Pg. iii

    Introduction   Pg. viii

1 **Whosoever Shall Call**   Pg. 1
    By Grace Through Faith and a Prayer?
    Behold me, Behold me
    Missing the Forest for the Trees
    Confession is Made unto Salvation
    Whosoever Shall Call

2 **Repentance Toward God and Faith** Pg. 31
    Toward Christ
    Without Faith It is Impossible
    Who Will Be God in Our Lives?
    Be Ye Reconciled to God

3 **The Hearing of Faith**   Pg. 53
    The Parable of the Sower
    Unbelief to Belief?

4 **Do Our Converts Glorify God?**   Pg. 73
    Questioning Our Fruits
    Sowing and Reaping

5 **Be Ye Holy**   Pg. 85
    The Disciple is not Above His Master
    O Wretched Man that I am

6 **The Beginning of Wisdom**   Pg. 99
    Bible as Our Example
    Modern Philosophy
    Underdeveloped Prefrontal Cortex
    Biblical Children's Ministries

7 **Sowing the Incorruptible Seed**   Pg. 127
    What is the Gospel Message?
    The Prodigal Son
    Looking for Evidences of Repentance
    Those Who Receive the Word Gladly

8	**Assurance of Salvation**	Pg. 145
	Convinced by a Preponderance of Evidence?	
	What Salvation Looks Like?	
	Biblical Assurances of Salvation	
9	**Continuation**	Pg. 159
	Chastening	
	Discerning Continuation in Children	
10	**Putting it Into Practice**	Pg. 165
	Opportunities for Evangelism	
	Conversation Starters,	
	Avoiding Rabbit Trails	
	Do's and Don'ts	
	Resources	
	Conclusion	Pg. 185

INTRODUCTION

Ever since the day I was saved, it has been my overwhelming desire to share the wonderful news of the gospel with others. To have the Holy Spirit of Christ within, and to be saved from condemnation and destruction of sin is the number one greatest thing that has ever happened in my life. I have at times, literally been busting to tell others of this life-changing gospel!

In my years as a Christian, everything I've sought to learn has been to that end. My studies and my desire to share spiritual truths, however, are not to become a theologian, teacher, pastor or a leader in the church. My only desire is to understand and share the gospel in the most biblical way I can; and if what I've learned can be of benefit to others' evangelistic efforts through this little book, then I pray the Lord will bless it.

In the beginning of my walk with the Lord, I went soul winning with everyone I could. For several years, I only watched and listened, learning simple methods of sharing the gospel such as the Roman's road and the ABC's of salvation, eventually leading many through prayers without much genuine evidence of faith. Often those I led through prayers showed little interest in God or his offer of salvation, yet I pushed for those prayers and decisions and counted them as salvations. Lord forgive me.

I continued to study the word as well as works of renowned Evangelists- George Whitfield, Charles Finney, Billy Sunday as well as more recent soul winners. I tried many methods of presenting salvation, such as Bill Bright's Four Spiritual Laws, Jack Hyles' salesman techniques, ...etc.

What I've learned through these many years of study and experience has convinced me that what we need is to seriously re-evaluate our soul-winning methods from the very foundation, putting aside our traditions and philosophies, and realigning ourselves with the precious word of God.

If we are ambassadors for Christ, commissioned to carry the greatest message ever told, we need to make sure we are doing it with the utmost diligence. I doubt that anyone reading this, desires to corrupt the gospel message, yet it is not hard to do if we hold to traditions rather than the word of God. I hope that anyone reading will seriously strive to see the difference and seek the way of truth.

Let me assure you that I'm not offering any new doctrines, only old truths, long forgotten by modern Christianity. I pray that these reminders are put together in a way that we can understand and apply them to a more biblical evangelism.

CHAPTER 1
WHOSOEVER SHALL CALL

"Whosoever shall call upon the name of the Lord shall be saved." (Romans 10:13)

It doesn't matter where you're from or who you are. No nation, race or even gender is excluded from this marvelous offer to all who will call upon the name of the Lord.

The question is: what does it mean to call upon the name of the Lord? Many today, teach that calling upon the name of the Lord means that a lost sinner must verbally confess their belief through prayer in order to be saved. It is often explained that we believe, but that believing isn't enough; we must receive salvation through prayer.

I recently read a little book by a very popular author. It was an evangelistic work geared toward explaining salvation to the lost. A friend of mine recommended it and shared that she planned to buy several in order to give them to those she was seeking to win for Christ. So, I excitedly downloaded it. I was thrilled with the explanation of how all the other religions of the world are works, or things to do, to achieve salvation, while Christianity alone stands on the fact that Christ has already *done* everything necessary for us to be saved. I rejoiced in so many truths so clearly explained, until it came to the point of explaining how we receive this gift of salvation offered freely to us through faith in Christ.

It was then that the Author undermined his own message with instructions of what to *do* to receive salvation. He suggested that faith in Christ is just the beginning, or first step, but that it does not actually secure salvation for us. He went on to instruct the reader that in order to accept this gift, they must also pray in order to receive Christ. He then suggested a sinner's prayer to use and assured the reader that if they had just prayed that prayer, that they are now indeed saved, clearly making prayer the instrument of salvation, rather than faith.

According to this philosophy, saving faith does not actually save; it is the prayer or confession that secures salvation. This has become a common teaching in Bible believing churches today; but where do we find this in Scripture? I'm sure that many of you reading this are thinking, "Well, isn't that what Romans 10:9-13 says?" But does this passage really teach that our prayer secures salvation for us?

Can we honestly reconcile this doctrine of securing salvation by a prayer with the rest of Scripture? Are we saved by grace through faith *and* our prayer?

The Bible tells us:

"For by grace are ye saved **through faith;** and that **not of yourselves**: it is the gift of God: Not of works, lest any man should boast." (Ephesians 2:8 & 9)

God's word says that it is *by grace through faith* (belief) that we are saved and that faith cometh by hearing.

"In whom ye also trusted, after that **ye heard the word of truth,** the gospel of your salvation: in whom also **after that ye believed**, **ye were sealed with that holy Spirit** of promise," (Ephesians 1:13)

"This only would I learn of you, **Received ye the Spirit** by the works of the law, or **by the hearing of faith?**" (Galatians 3:2)

Do we receive the Holy Spirit of Christ by the hearing of faith, as the word says, or by praying a sinner's prayer? According to the word, we receive the Spirit through faith, *not* through praying a prayer.

> "That the blessing of Abraham might come on the Gentiles through Jesus Christ; **that we might receive the promise of the Spirit through faith**." (Galatians 3:14)

It is *God's word* that saves not man's own words through a prayer.

> "Being born again, not of corruptible seed, but of incorruptible, **by the word of God,** which liveth and abideth for ever." (1 Peter 1:23)

Receiving salvation through prayer was *not* the method or message of the Apostles, or of the early church. The Sinner's Prayer itself is a modern invention, dating back only to the mid-twentieth century. The timing and emergence of the Sinner's Prayer type of evangelism is clearly documented in historical biblical and evangelistic literature produced over the last couple hundred years, proving that the Sinner's Prayer did not exist prior to the 1940's-1950's.

It was introduced in its most basic form by Billy Graham as a closing thought to his "Four Steps to Peace with God" tract and further developed and implemented by Bill Bright in his tract entitled "The Four Spiritual Laws".

Author Thomas Ross references Dr. Paul Chitwood's 2001 Ph.D. dissertation in the article The Sinners Prayer: A Historical and Theological Analysis, Southern Baptist Theological Seminary 2001. (Ross, Thomas. "The Sinners Prayer: A Historical and Theological Analysis." Faith Saves, 17 June 2017)

Quoting Dr. Chitwood:

> "The Sinner's Prayer represents an unmistakable and dramatic shift in the theology of evangelism . . . the Sinner's prayer did not appear until well into the twentieth century . . . Moreover, the concept of bringing or inviting "Jesus into your heart" is one that does not occur readily before the turn of the twentieth century. . . to think that we cannot lead a person to

Christ without the prayer is a mistaken assumption . . . The transition to a systematized presentation and a standardized prayer can be seen in the evangelistic literature and training manuals of the early twentieth century. . ."

"[T]he process of getting saved in America has changed considerably since Jonathan Edwards placed sinners in the hand of an angry God. . . [T]he origin of this concept of conversion [can be traced] to the Christian (Plymouth) Brethren of the nineteenth century. . . The Brethren . . . stressed the concept of "receiving" Christ, thought of feelings as being irrelevant in conversion, and downplayed repentance. . . The stress on mere intellectual acceptance of the gospel naturally yielded an evangelistic appeal that sought an instant "decision" for Christ. . . Often in the counseling room the inquirer was just asked, "Do you accept Jesus as your Savior?", and when the person said, "Yes!", as most did, that individual was immediately regarded as converted. . . The "decisionism" concept of conversion was epitomized in the evangelism of Finney. . . [T]he conversion process shortened substantially. The lengthy struggles with sin and self that characterized earlier Regular and separate Baptist conversion were reduced to sign posts on the way to instantaneous regeneration. Conversion became a simple matter of praying the "sinners prayer" and inviting Jesus into your heart. One sincere prayer brought immediate salvation." (Ross, Thomas. "The Sinners Prayer: A Historical and Theological Analysis." Faith Saves, 17 June 2017)

Along with this transition toward a prayer as the means of receiving salvation, came the change from calling lost sinners to repent of their sin and seek reconciliation with God through Christ's sacrificial death, to a plea for the lost to merely make a decision to *accept Christ* or *ask him into their hearts*. This may not seem like a big deal to those who have become comfortably familiar with this terminology; but think for a moment about the magnitude of that statement.

Christ, the sinless Son of God left his throne in Heaven, suffered humiliation and cruel torture, died, was buried, and rose again to pay the debt of sin that we owe in order to reconcile us to our holy God. Instead of repentant sinners throwing themselves at the foot of the cross for mercy from God, our modern gospel calls for them to merely accept Christ. Most often, these unrepentant sinners are offered a place in Heaven with God if they will simply pray a prayer to invite Jesus into their sinful hearts, as though they are doing Christ a favor.

This is a far cry from broken repentant sinners clinging to the precious Savior who has snatched them from the brink of Hell. Is it any wonder our converts find it so easy to continue in sin or fall back into it so quickly when, most often, they have never even understood the cost?

Because this method has been taught for the last two or three generations, I understand that it may be difficult for those who have grown up in this mindset to let go of these traditions. Many in leadership today are those who were themselves evangelized according to this philosophy.

There may also be a measure of emotional investment for those who currently lead ministries and already have a long list of souls they have dealt with according to these teachings. More than likely, family members are numbered among them. I pray that the sincere love for souls and desire to genuinely please God will enable us to look past tradition to the truth of the word.

No matter what we have been taught, or believed, if it goes against the truth of the word, we must allow God's word to be our final authority. If what we are teaching does not line up with the truth we see in Scripture, we must accept that it is not God's word that is wrong. Will we hearken to the word of God, or to the words of men according to commentaries and evangelists?

"He that hath ears to hear, let him hear." (Matthew 11:15)

If the Bible does not tell us that we must pray and ask Christ to save us, then we may be in danger of serious error.

> Bible uses words like "call upon" and confess w/ thy mouth

Adding requirements to salvation that the Bible does not is no less than adding works to the gospel. If the Bible does not tell sinners that they must pray to be saved, then are we not guilty of preaching another gospel?

During Christ's time on earth, we are told of many who came to faith in him, but *none* that were commanded by him to pray in order to receive salvation.

> all examples of Pre-atonement salvation

To the sinful woman who washed his feet with her hair, Jesus simply said, "... Thy faith hath saved thee; go in peace" (Luke 7:50). There is nothing to indicate that she prayed any prayer or asked him to save her, but only her faith is mentioned here.

To the woman with the issue of blood, who reached out and touched his garment he said: "Daughter, be of good comfort; thy faith hath made thee whole" (Matthew 9:22). Again, there is no indication that she had said a prayer of any sort.

The Samaritan woman at the well was saved while speaking with the Lord, and yet, once again no prayer is mentioned and no asking him into her heart or life. (John 4:1-42) As a matter of fact, when she claimed to even want the water of life, she was yet unaware of who Christ was. She certainly could not have been praying to him as her Savior.

The list could go on and on of those who simply believed without profession or prayer: Zaccheus, the centurion's servant, the man who was sick with palsy, whose friends brought him to Christ…etc.

Repentant faith is certainly described in all these accounts, but not a word is ever recorded about a Sinner's prayer or any prayer at all being used as a means of receiving salvation.

We receive the regenerating Holy Spirit by the

hearing of faith, being born again by the Word of God.

That might seem like a lot to wrap our heads around, but it is vitally important that we understand this if we are going to share the message of salvation biblically.

> "Because strait is the gate, and narrow is the way, which leadeth unto life, and few there be that find it." (Matthew 7:14)

The truth of salvation is so narrow that veering too far to the left or to the right can easily lead our converts *away* from salvation. Modern evangelism leans so far toward obtaining decisions and prayers that the preaching of the gospel is usually neglected. Many reduce it to a bare-bones presentation of the facts of Christ's death, burial, and resurrection, even bragging about presenting it in under thirty seconds. This certainly was not the case with Paul or the other apostles. We read that at times, they reasoned with the lost for days.

Securing decisions and prayers, can easily take priority over sowing and watering the seed of the word. Our aim should be to lead people, through the preaching of the word, to repentance toward God and a genuine faith toward Jesus Christ. If our goal is seeking after a prayer, then often, that's all we get.

> "They profess that they know God; but in works they deny him, being abominable, and disobedient, and unto every good work reprobate." (Titus 1:16)

Of course, we are anxious for people to receive Christ as Savior, but how does the Bible say we receive him? *By believing.* A person who has truly come to a knowledge of the truth and believed *will* confess Christ; but it is *by belief* that we receive him, not by a decision or prayer.

> "But **as many as received him**, to them gave he power to become the sons of God, even to **them that believe on his name**:" (John 1:12)

This verse is often used to encourage a decision or prayer. Receiving Christ is presented as an action or decision, but the word of God defines for itself, what it means to receive Christ. Those who receive him are those that *believe* on his name.

Romans Chapter 10

Since the Scriptures are clear that praying a prayer is not necessary in order to secure salvation, there must be some misunderstanding regarding our interpretation of Romans 10:9-13.

In order to understand "For whosoever shall call upon the name of the Lord shall be saved…" (Romans 10:13) accurately, we must again, allow Scripture to interpret itself, comparing spiritual with spiritual, and viewing it in its proper context.

I believe that as Gentiles we often view Scripture from a strictly Gentile perspective, seeking what God has for, or is saying to us the church, even divorcing New Testament Scriptures from their Old Testament references. This narrow perspective has led to an improper interpretation and application of Romans Chapter 10:9-13.

We have zeroed in on these few verses and simply missed the forest for the trees.

In spite of the fact that *calling upon the name of the Lord* in prayer as the catalyst for receiving salvation is not exampled anywhere else in the New Testament, "Whosoever shall call upon the name of the Lord shall be saved" (Romans 10:13) has become the foundation for the evangelism methods we practice today.

The Scripture being referenced here is in fact from the Old Testament book of Joel and was not a prayer for individual salvation, but a promise of deliverance from end-time destruction during the seventieth week, for a remnant of faithful Jewish believers in God.

> "And it shall come to pass, that whosoever shall call on the name of the LORD shall be delivered: for in mount Zion and in Jerusalem shall be deliverance, as the LORD hath said, and in the remnant whom the LORD shall call." (Joel 2:32)

Chapter ten of the book of Romans is an amazing picture of God's grace and mercy toward us, but more than that it is a message of hope for the Jewish people as well. When we step back and look at the big picture, we see an entirely different significance to this passage, one that glorifies God.

[margin notes: yes, that Jews also may partake of salvation — the mystery not known to Jews]

The truths revealed through this chapter alone, have at times brought me to tears, because of his great love.

Romans 10: 1-14

> "Brethren, my heart's desire and prayer to God for Israel is, that they might be saved. For I bear them record that they have a zeal of God, but not according to knowledge. For they being ignorant of God's righteousness, and going about to establish their own righteousness, have not submitted themselves unto the righteousness of God. For Christ is the end of the law for righteousness to every one that believeth. For Moses describeth the righteousness which is of the law, That the man which doeth those things shall live by them. But the righteousness which is of faith speaketh on this wise, **Say not in thine heart, Who shall ascend into**

heaven? (that is, to bring Christ down from above:) Or, Who shall descend into the deep? (that is, to bring up Christ again from the dead.) But what saith it? The word is nigh thee, even in thy mouth, and in thy heart: that is, the word of faith, which we preach; That if thou shalt confess with thy mouth the Lord Jesus, and shalt believe in thine heart that God hath raised him from the dead, thou shalt be saved. For with the heart man believeth unto righteousness; and <u>with the mouth confession is made unto salvation</u>. For the Scripture saith, Whosoever believeth on him shall not be ashamed. For there is no difference between the Jew and the Greek: for the same Lord over all is rich unto all that call upon him. For whosoever shall call upon the name of the Lord shall be saved. How then shall they call on him in whom they have not believed? and how shall they believe in him of whom they have not heard? and how shall they hear without a preacher?" (Romans 10:1-14)

The apostle Paul begins this chapter with a continuation of his discussion of his Jewish brethren who have stumbled and not attained to the law of righteousness that they had sought.

Romans 10:1

"Brethren, my heart's desire and prayer to God for Israel is, that they might be saved." (Romans 10:1)

Paul is speaking of his desire for the salvation of his Jewish brethren. This is the context by which we must understand this passage. Speaking of them, he tells us that they have "a zeal of God, but not according to knowledge." (v.2) The Jews, as God's people, have sought to establish their own righteousness through the law and have sadly failed to see their long-awaited Savior who offers them his own perfect righteousness instead.

Romans 10:4

"For Christ is the end of the law for righteousness to every one that believeth." (Romans 10:4)

To understand the situation fully, we must first review a little of the background information. We know that God had called the people of Israel, to be his people, to worship and glorify him, and show his great power and mercy to all the world. God promised to bless them if they would simply obey him and curse them if they would not.

"Behold, I set before you this day a blessing and a curse; A blessing, if ye obey the commandments of the LORD your God, which I command you this day: And a curse, if ye will not obey the commandments of the LORD your God, but turn aside out of the way which I command you this day, to go after other gods, which ye have not known." (Deuteronomy 11:26-28)

As God's chosen people, they were to obey all that he commanded, and in so doing, glorify his name; *but they would not*. This promise was not only for one generation or group of believers at one point in time; but, as God's chosen line, they were to each choose this in every generation. Some would believe and choose good for a while and follow the Lord.

At other times entire generations would choose evil and turn from him in disobedience. Those who would not repent and call upon the name of the Lord for deliverance, returning to him as his people would be punished for their sin, and endure his wrath, often leaving only a believing remnant. This was a continuing pattern for their nation.

No matter how many times God reached out his hand of mercy toward them, revealing more of his goodness and love, they would once again turn a blind eye to him, stopping their ears, and refusing to hear or obey him. They hardened their hearts against him and refused to be faithful. Instead, they would once again run off to worship and serve other gods. Is it any wonder God tired of offering himself to them?

Because of this continuing disobedience, God's divine judgment fell upon them. He gave them the spiritual blindness and hardness of heart they had been practicing for so long. Think about that for a moment.

"For the LORD hath poured out upon you the spirit of deep sleep, and hath closed your eyes: the prophets and your rulers, the seers hath he covered. And the vision of all is become unto you as the words of a book that is sealed, which men deliver to one that is learned, saying, Read this, I pray thee: and he saith, I cannot; for it is sealed: And the book is delivered to him that is not learned, saying, Read this, I pray thee: and he saith, I am not learned. Wherefore the Lord said, Forasmuch as **this people draw near me with their mouth, and with their lips do honour me, but have removed their heart far from me, and their fear toward me is taught by the precept of men:"** (Isaiah 29:10-13)

Because they hardened their hearts against God, provoking him continually by their worship of other gods, God blinded them and would now provoke *them* to jealousy by offering *himself* to a people who were not his people, the Gentiles. This place of spiritual blindness is where we find the Jews that Paul is speaking of. Throughout the book of Romans, and especially here in chapter ten, Paul quotes Old Testament Scripture, setting the tone and the context for the message he is giving. All caps indicate direct quotes from the Old Testament.

Romans 10:19

"But I say, Did not Israel know? First Moses saith, I WILL PROVOKE YOU TO JEALOUSY BY THEM THAT ARE NO PEOPLE, AND BY A FOOLISH NATION I WILL ANGER YOU." (Romans 10:19 All caps indicate Old Testament references) This is a quote from Isaiah 32:21

Paul continues in Romans 10:20-21 with a reference from Isaiah 65:1-2

"But Esaias is very bold, and saith, I WAS FOUND OF THEM THAT SOUGHT ME NOT, I WAS MADE MANIFEST UNTO THEM THAT ASKED NOT AFTER ME. But to Israel he saith, ALL THE DAY LONG I HAVE STRETCHED FORTH MY HANDS UNTO A DISOBEDIENT AND GAINSAYING PEOPLE." (All caps indicate Old Testament references)

Behold me, Behold me

This sad assessment of Israel's failure is even more heartbreaking in Isaiah's account.

"I am sought of them that asked not for me; I am found of them that sought me not: I said, **Behold me, behold me**, unto a nation that was not called by my name. I have spread out my hands all the day unto a rebellious people, which walketh in a way that was not good, after their own thoughts; A people that provoketh me to anger continually to my face; that sacrificeth in gardens, and burneth incense upon altars of brick; (Isaiah 65:1-3)

Because Israel refused to look to him and glorify him alone, God calls to the Gentile world, "Behold me, behold me." (I don't know about you, but that statement by God overwhelms my heart every time I read it.)

God, in his desire to reconcile man to himself, said "Behold me, behold me," and showed himself to the entire world in the flesh as Jesus Christ. He offered himself to the Gentiles and they *would* look to him.

God became man and dwelt among us so that the entire world would see his glory and be drawn to him; all but the Jews, that is. Because of their blindness, seeing Christ, they would not be able to see who he was. Hearing, they would not hear or understand the message of salvation.

Throughout the Old Testament we see Jehovah God revealing different aspects of himself through his names such as Elohim, the strong one, El Shaddai, the strong one who strengthens, Jehovah Jireh, the Lord will provide, and Jehovah Rah, the Lord is my shepherd, just to name a few.

God now reveals himself to the world by a new name, Immanuel, God with us.

> "Therefore the Lord himself shall give you a sign; Behold, a virgin shall conceive, and bear a son, and shall call his name Immanuel." (Isaiah 7:14)

Those who are willing to turn to the Father, to hear and to see him, come to him now through Jesus (meaning Jehovah is salvation), rather than through the sacrifices of the law. Believers in God would now be called Christians as followers of Christ.

> "… he that hath seen me hath seen the Father; and how sayest thou then, Shew us the Father?" (John 14:9)

> "Jesus saith unto him, I am the way, the truth, and the life: no man cometh unto the Father, but by me." (John 14:6)

Although God desired to show his glory to the world through the Jews, they *refused* to honor him. Instead they shamed his name by their wicked disobedience and gave the glory that belonged to him, to other gods.

God then showed himself to the world through Jesus Christ and now calls the Gentiles to be *his people*, to glorify him and carry his message of reconciliation to the rest of the world. As believers, our lives are not our own to do as we please, but are a purchased possession of God, to be used for his glory. Although we are not under the law as the Jews, we *are* called to be *holy as God is holy*, a *set apart, peculiar* people, who *will* glorify his name. Those who are born again by the Holy Spirit of Christ and freed from the bondage of sin, *desire* the things of God and glory in him.

> "And hereby we do know that we know him, if we keep his commandments. **He that saith, I know him, and keepeth not his commandments, is a liar**, and the truth is not in him." (1 John 2:3-4)

Yet today, it is difficult to see *any* difference between professing Christians and the world. Spiritually, physically, morally, we just don't seem to be doing any better than the Jews in glorifying his name.

The Jews Paul speaks of in this passage of Romans *could not* come to God through Jesus because they were now blinded to the truth of his identity (all but the faithful remnant). What then must his brethren do? If they have killed their Savior and have stumbled at the point of faith, not attaining to righteousness, how might they yet be saved? Is it too late for them? Is forgiveness and reconciliation with God beyond reach?

In verses Romans 10:5-8, Paul attempts to answer these unspoken questions by drawing attention to the Old Testament instructions that God gave to them through Moses, promises of deliverance should they wander away from him.

Romans 10:5-8

"For Moses describeth the righteousness which is of the law, That the man which doeth those things shall live by them. But the righteousness which is of faith speaketh on this wise, SAY NOT IN THINE HEART, WHO SHALL ASCEND INTO HEAVEN? (that is, to bring Christ down from above OR, WHO SHALL ASCEND INTO THE DEEP? (that is, to bring up Christ again from the dead.) But what saith it? THE WORD IS NIGH THEE EVEN IN THY MOUTH, AND IN THY HEART: that is, the word of faith, which we preach;" (Romans 10:5-8) (All caps indicate Old Testament references.) This portion is from Deuteronomy 30:10-16

"**If thou shalt hearken unto the voice of the LORD thy God, to keep his commandments and his statutes** which are written in this book of the law, and if thou **turn unto the LORD thy God with all thine heart, and with all thy soul.** For **this commandment which I command thee this day, it is not hidden from thee, neither is it far off.** It is not in heaven, that thou shouldest say, Who shall go up for us to heaven, and bring it unto us, that we may hear it, and do it? Neither is it beyond the sea, that thou shouldest say, Who shall go over the sea for us, and bring it unto us, that we may hear it, and do it? **But the word is very nigh unto thee, in thy mouth, and in thy heart, that thou mayest do it.** See, I have set before thee this day life and good, and death and evil; In that **I command thee this day to love the LORD thy God, to walk in his ways, and to keep his commandments and his statutes and his judgments**, that thou mayest live and multiply: and the LORD thy God shall bless thee in the land whither thou goest to possess it." (Deuteronomy 30:10-16)

The commandment that is nigh in their mouth and in

their hearts is the commandment we just read above, to "hearken unto the voice of the LORD thy God, to keep his commandments and his statutes…" and to "turn unto the LORD thy God with all thine heart, and with all thy soul". (Deuteronomy 30:10)

Paul is using Scripture that would be very familiar to his Jewish brethren, speaking of God's warning that when they would wander away into sin and disobedience, he would punish them by sending his curses upon them. If, however, they would turn from their sin and rebellion, and return to him with all their hearts he would once again embrace them and bless them and deliver them from his wrath.

This is not salvation by works Paul is speaking of, but a sincere turning to God from their wicked, idolatrous disobedience. It is repentance that is commanded.

"And the LORD thy God will make thee plenteous in every work of thine hand, in the fruit of thy body, and in the fruit of thy cattle, and in the fruit of thy land, for good: for the LORD will again rejoice over thee for good, as he rejoiced over thy fathers: **If thou shalt hearken unto the voice of the LORD thy God**, to keep his commandments and his statutes which are written in this book of the law, **and if thou turn unto the LORD thy God with all thine heart,** and with all thy soul." (Deuteronomy 30: 9-10)

This command, to turn back to him in repentance, he reminds them is *not hidden*, or difficult, *neither is it far away* that they should have to send someone to go and bring the message to them. God says it is near to them, *even nigh in their mouths and in their hearts*. What he is saying is that this message is so familiar to them, that it should not even need to be repeated. They *know* the answer. For them to miss it, would only be willful ignorance and continued rejection of his word.

"But **if** from thence **thou shalt seek the LORD thy God,** thou shalt find him, **if** thou seek him with all thy heart and with all thy soul. When thou art in tribulation, and all these things are come upon thee, even in the latter days, **if thou turn to the LORD thy God, and shalt be obedient unto his voice;"** (Deuteronomy 4:29-30)

Paul says it is the same now. The message of salvation is not far from the Jews. It is not an unattainable feat that they cannot accomplish. The message is so near that it is even in their mouths.

The answer is repentance toward God and faith in Jesus Christ, the same message they have already heard, but sadly, because of their continual unwillingness to hearken to God, are now blinded and deafened to; seeing they see not and hearing they hear not.

Jesus, quoting Isaiah references this present blindness:

"For **this people's heart is waxed gross,** and **their ears are dull of hearing,** and **their eyes they have closed; lest at any time they should** see with their eyes, and hear with their ears, and should understand with their heart, **and should be converted,** and I should heal them." (Matthew 13:15)

Jesus, in this passage from Matthew was rebuking Israel for their insincere worship and refusal to obey. Although they have heard God's promises over and over, they do not listen to or obey him and have willingly closed their eyes to his commands. Because of this, their hearts are fat with ignorance and disobedience. Their worship is not sincere, but hypocritical, seeking to establish their own righteousness through the sacrifices of the law rather than to offer God the sacrifices of a broken and contrite spirit. They offered to God, not their obedience, but their works.

In Romans chapter eleven we see Paul ask the Question: "I say then, Hath God cast away his people? God forbid." (Romans 11:1)

> "Behold therefore the goodness and severity of God: on them which fell, severity; but toward thee, goodness, if thou continue in his goodness: otherwise thou also shalt be cut off. And they also, if they abide not still in unbelief, shall be graffed in: for God is able to graff them in again." (Romans 11:22-23)

Even the Jews, if they will not abide still in unbelief can be grafted in once again. How? The answer is the same as it's always been, by turning to God in repentance of their sin and rebellion and believing in God who is now seen in the person of Jesus Christ (the rock of offense, the stone of stumbling, Immanuel, God with us).

> "To wit, that God was in Christ, reconciling the world unto himself, not imputing their trespasses unto them; **and hath committed unto us the word of reconciliation.**" (2 Corinthians 5:19)

Just as Moses set before them the choice to obey or disobey, the choice of life or death; so, Paul sets the same choice before them. If they are willing to turn from their sin and be reconciled to God, they too can believe in Christ (God manifested in the flesh) and be saved. If not, then they will continue in their blindness toward Christ.

> "But **if ye turn unto me**, and keep my commandments, and do them; though there were of you cast out unto the uttermost part of the heaven, yet will I gather them from thence, and will bring them unto the place that I have chosen to set my name there."

(Nehemiah 1:9)

Paul goes on to explain that if they will turn back to God and believe in the sacrifice he has provided through Jesus Christ, confessing Christ as the fulfillment of the New Covenant, they can yet be saved.

Romans 10:9-10

"That if thou shalt confess with thy mouth the Lord Jesus, and shalt believe in thine heart that God hath raised him from the dead, thou shalt be saved For with the heart man believeth unto righteousness; and with the mouth confession is made unto salvation." (Romans 10:9-10)

Many equate this confession with a prayer, insisting that one must pray in order to be saved. Confession has a distinctly different meaning than prayer.

Confession: According to Strong's Exhaustive Concordance of the Bible, ὁμολογέω homologéō, hom-ol-og-eh'-o; from a compound of the base of G3674 and G3056: is defined as follows: **to assent, i.e. covenant**, acknowledge:—con-(pro-)fess, confession is made, give thanks, promise. (Strong's Greek Lexicon (KJV)." Blue Letter Bible. Web. 28 Sep, 2019.)

Notice that confession is not a one-time verbal prayer. Those who confessed or *pro*fessed Jehovah in the Old Testament were those who associated themselves with him as his followers, his covenant people. Likewise, confessing Christ implies the idea of a public acknowledgement of or covenanting with him as his followers.

Confession is *not* a lost person asking for salvation, merely speaking the name of Christ as a magical prayer or incantation. It is a saved person declaring their relationship with him, confessing his name as his follower.

Confessing Christ was certainly not to be empty words, honoring him with their lips while their hearts remained far from him, but genuine heart belief demonstrated by the public acknowledging of Christ, even to the hazarding of their own lives.

Whosoever confessed Christ must not only accept that this Jesus was truly their long-awaited Savior that they had crucified, but the sure foundation for all that they believe.

Romans 10:11

"For the Scripture saith, WHOSOEVER BELIEVETH ON HIM SHALL NOT BE ASHAMED." (Romans 10:11) (All caps indicate Old Testament references)

This verse begins with *For*, showing that it is a continuation of the previous thought: "...With the mouth confession is made unto salvation *FOR* the Scripture saith, whosoever believeth shall not be ashamed." (Romans 10:10-11) Secret belief just would not do. God was calling for unashamed acknowledgement as worshippers of Christ.

This verse references Isaiah where God speaks to the wicked rulers of Israel who have made a covenant with death and Hell.

"Therefore thus saith the Lord GOD, Behold, I lay in Zion for a foundation a stone, a tried stone, a precious corner stone, a sure foundation: he that believeth **shall not make haste**." (Isaiah 28:16)

Because they had turned their backs on God in such wicked disobedience, he told them that Jesus Christ would be to them a stone of stumbling. He that believeth *shall not make haste* suggests making a hasty departure or fleeing in shame. So, Paul reminds them that whosoever believeth shall not be ashamed.

Those who confessed the name of Jehovah God or *called upon the name of the Lord* in the Old Testament were his covenant people, those who worshipped God. We, as Christians, come to God through Christ, the author of the New Covenant.

For the Jews, the greatest obstacle in their path was confessing that Christ truly was their long-awaited Savior, that they had rejected. God laid this foundation stone, a precious corner stone, which to the Jews has become a stone of stumbling.

Confessing Christ at this point in history, was not only humbling, but quite possibly the most dangerous thing they could choose to do. This had the potential to not only force them from their synagogues, but also to endanger their lives. For them, confessing to be worshippers of Christ was a big commitment to make.

It was not their entrance into salvation but was testimony unto their salvation and a new covenant relationship with Christ. Confessing Christ, publicly acknowledging themselves as his followers was a test of their faith.

Confession is made *unto* salvation, not *into* salvation

Many Christians read this verse and understand it to mean that confession is made *into* salvation; but we see that confession is made *unto* salvation. Confession does not *make us* saved it is the *testimony* of our salvation.

The word **unto** in Strong's Exhaustive Concordance of the Bible is: Eis G1519 The KJV translates Strong's G1519 in the following manner: into (573x), to (281x), unto (207x), for (140x), in (138x), on (58x), toward (29x), against (26x), miscellaneous (322x). into, unto, to, towards, for, among. (Strong's Greek Lexicon (KJV)." Blue Letter Bible. Web. 28

Sep, 2019.)

While it can also mean *into,* which it is translated as five hundred and seventy-three times; that is not how it has been translated here. Because of the context in which it is used, it is translated and understood as *unto*. Here we see the same word, unto used in Matthew 8:5, translated *into* in the first part of the verse and *unto* in the second.

> "And when Jesus was entered **into** (same word G1519) Capernaum, there came **unto** (same word G1519) him a centurion, beseeching him," (Matthew 8:5)

The exact same word *unto*, is used by John the Baptist.

> "I indeed baptize you with water **unto** repentance: but he that cometh after me is mightier than I, whose shoes I am not worthy to bear: he shall baptize you with the Holy Ghost, and with fire:" (Matthew 3:11)

John baptized *unto* repentance toward God, "preparing the way of the Lord, turning the hearts of the fathers to the children, and the disobedient to the wisdom of the just; to make ready a people prepared for the Lord." (Luke 1:17)

John's baptism was not *into* repentance, meaning that the act of baptism placed them into repentance. John called for fruits appropriate for repentance to be evident prior to baptism. Those who were baptized came confessing their sins.

> "But when he saw many of the Pharisees and Sadducees come to his baptism, he said unto them, O generation of vipers, who hath warned you to flee from the wrath to come? Bring forth therefore fruits meet for repentance:" (Matthew 3:7-8)

The act of baptism was not considered to *be* repentance, neither did it secure repentance. It simply testified *unto* their repentance. It is the same with confession. Confession is made *unto* the salvation that has already been received by faith. It is not an added requirement for salvation.

To some, it may not seem like a big deal to present a prayer as a means of entering into salvation; but anytime we are attempting to add anything other than faith to salvation, (as in adding a prayer to faith) we are walking on very dangerous ground.

Telling someone that they must pray a prayer in order to be saved is no different than telling them that they must be baptized to be saved.

If we are to interpret the Scripture "confession is made unto salvation" (Romans 10:10), as teaching that salvation is secured by our confession (through prayer); we would have to then also interpret "he that believeth and is baptized shall be saved..." (Mark 16:16) the same way.

We know that Scripture interprets Scripture best and our answer is found in the verses that follow each of these examples.

"He that believeth and is baptized shall be saved; **but he that believeth not shall be damned**." (Mark 16:16)

The key element is clearly belief. Without belief, there is no salvation. Baptism is only a testimony of salvation, *not* that which *secures* salvation. It is the same with confession, which is clarified by the verses that follow as well.

"How then shall they call on him in whom they have not believed?" (Romans 10:14)

The Scripture asks: how can they call if they have not

believed? Calling, or confessing without belief also equals damnation.

"For with the heart man believeth unto righteousness;" (Romans 10:10)

One cannot call upon the Lord without belief. So, we see the same scenario: He that believes, and calls is saved. He that believes not, and calls is damned. It is not confession that secures salvation; it is belief.

"How then shall they call on him in whom they have not believed? and how shall they believe in him of whom they have not heard? and how shall they hear without a preacher? And how shall they preach, except they be sent? as it is written, How beautiful are the feet of them that preach the gospel of peace and bring glad tidings of good things!" (Romans 10:14-15).

How can they believe if they have not heard? They cannot call, without first believing. Calling requires belief→ Belief requires hearing→ Hearing requires preaching.

Although we are commanded to be baptized as a testimony to our salvation, we know that baptism does not secure salvation and that we *can* be saved without being baptized. The same way, we are commanded to confess, but the confession does not secure salvation; belief does.

While baptism and confession both show faith. They are merely evidences of genuine faith. Notice I said *evidences*, not proofs. Neither a profession nor a baptism is proof of salvation. It is the same thing James is speaking of when he says faith without works is dead.

"Yea, a man may say, Thou hast faith, and I have works: shew me thy faith without thy works, and I will shew thee my faith by my works." (James 2:18)

True faith will have works. The public confession is one of the tests of sincerity. Someone who is not willing to publicly embrace Christ, willingly aligning his life with Christ is probably not a sincere believer.

In the Old Testament, calling upon the name of the Lord was not used as a one-time verbal call for entrance into salvation.

Those who *called upon the name of the Lord* in the Old Testament did so from a position of willing association with God as his followers. They, as his covenant people were privileged to invoke the name of God in times of need. We see Paul use the same phrase to describe believers in Christ today.

"Unto the church of God which is at Corinth, to them that are sanctified in Christ Jesus, called to be saints, with **all that in every place call upon the name of Jesus Christ our Lord**, both theirs and ours:" (1 Corinthians 1:2)

According to Strong's concordance of the Bible, (Strong's Greek Lexicon "G1941 - epikaleō - Strong's Greek Lexicon (KJV)." Blue Letter Bible, the phrase **call upon the name of the Lord,** is an expression finding its explanation in the fact that prayers addressed to God ordinarily began with an invocation of the divine name, Jehovah. (Strong's Greek Lexicon (KJV)." Blue Letter Bible. Web. 28 Sep, 2019.)

Those who called upon (or petitioned) the name of the Lord were they who worshipped God- those who confessed his name.

Bensons Commentary of Genesis 4:26. And to Seth was born a son called Enos, which is the general name for all men, and speaks the weakness, frailty, and misery of man's state. Then began men to call upon the name of the Lord — Doubtless God's name was called upon before: but now, 1st,

The worshippers of God began to do more in religion than they had done; perhaps not more than had been done at first, but more than had been done since the defection of Cain. Now men began to worship God, not only in their closets and families, but in public and solemn assemblies. 2nd, The worshippers of God began to distinguish themselves: so the margin reads it. **Then began men to be called by the name of the Lord — or, to call themselves by it. Now Cain and those that had deserted religion had built a city, and begun to declare for irreligion, and called themselves the sons of men. Those that adhered to God began to declare for him and his worship and called themselves the sons of God.** (Benson's Commentary, Genesis, Bible Hub Wed. 28, Sept. 2019)

Calling upon the name of the Lord is exclusively used by believers, *not unbelievers*. It is not a prayer of the lost asking for salvation. In Romans 10:13 we see the promise of deliverance for those believers who call upon the Lord.

"For there is no difference between the Jew and the Greek: for the same Lord over all is rich unto all that call upon him. FOR WHOSOEVER SHALL CALL UPON THE NAME OF THE LORD SHALL BE SAVED. (Romans 10:12-13) (All caps indicate Old Testament references)

In this quote from Joel, this end time promise of deliverance was in the context of tribulation and persecution that would come with the Day of the Lord.

"And it shall come to pass, that **whosoever shall call on the name of the LORD shall be delivered**: for in mount Zion and in Jerusalem shall be deliverance…" (Joel 2:32)

During the seventieth week, the believing Jews who are called by his name, that look to him for help will be delivered them from their impending destruction and come to faith in Christ.

"And so all Israel shall be saved: as it is written, There shall come out of Sion the Deliverer, and shall turn away ungodliness from Jacob:" (Romans 11:26)

As we can see in the verses below, calling upon the name of the Lord was used not only as a declaration of themselves as his followers, but also as a petitioning of the name of the God they worshipped, Jehovah, in times of trouble or in the context of the returning to God by sinful believers who have gone astray.

"But Naaman was wroth, and went away, and said, Behold, I thought, He will surely come out to me, and stand, and **call on the name of the LORD** his God, and strike his hand over the place, and recover the leper."(2 Kings 5:11)

"When thy people Israel be smitten down before the enemy, because they have sinned against thee, and **shall turn again to thee, and confess thy name**, and pray, and make supplication unto thee in this house:" (1 Kings 8:33)

"And I will bring the third part through the fire, and will refine them as silver is refined, and will try them as gold is tried: they **shall call on my name**, and I will hear them: I will say, It is my people: and they shall say, The LORD is my God." (Zechariah 13:9)

"Give thanks unto the LORD, call upon his name, make known his deeds among the people."
(1 Chronicles 16:8)

"**I will call on the LORD**, who is worthy to be praised: so shall I be saved from mine enemies."
(2 Samuel 22:4)

> "When heaven is shut up, and there is no rain, because they have sinned against thee; if they pray toward this place, **and confess thy name**, and turn from their sin, when thou afflictest them:" (1 Kings 8:35)

The privilege of petitioning or *calling upon the name* of the Lord is now extended to believing Gentiles as well as Jews through salvation in Jesus.

Calling upon the name of the Lord is not a magic prayer to secure salvation.

Whether we are willing to admit it or not, we as Christians, have so missed the significance of *calling upon the name of the Lord*, that it is now nothing more than a magic prayer that is regularly offered to those who, like the rebellious Israelites, refuse to obey or to glorify God.

Modern Christianity preaches a message of *Just accept Jesus* or *ask him into your heart,* without preaching repentance from sin and encourages those who often have no interest in glorifying God, to receive salvation by simply speaking the Sinner's Prayer.

Why would we think that he would accept this lip-service without repentance from Gentiles when he would not accept it from the Jews, his chosen people? Jesus Christ is God in the flesh. Have we been so long in Christianity that we've forgotten who God is? We are simply without excuse.

"*Whosoever shall call upon the name of the Lord shall be saved*" is not a promise of salvation to whoever decides to pray a prayer. Without repentance toward God as well as genuine faith toward Christ, a sinner's prayer is worthless.

Just as Paul called his Jewish brethren to turn to God in repentance and place their faith in Christ, we must also call the lost to do the same.

CHAPTER 2
REPENTANCE TOWARD GOD AND FAITH TOWARD CHRIST

> "But Israel, which followed after the law of righteousness, hath not attained to the law of righteousness. Wherefore? Because they sought it not by faith, but as it were by the works of the law." (Romans 9:31-32)

The Jews did not attain to the righteousness they sought, because they sought it *not by faith*, but by the works of the law. That statement puzzled me for a long time. I wondered why, if they were faithfully holding to the law, repenting of sin and seeking to be righteous before God through the sacrifices of the law, they could not see the bigger picture. Why were they blinded if they were performing the works of the law as they were commanded?

The problem was that they were not seeking to be righteous before God, but merely righteous according to the law. Holding to the law became for them, a mere pretense of worship, making them righteous in their own eyes while they continued in their sin against God.

As his chosen people, God gave them everything they could ever desire and more, showing them his great love and mercy and even made provision for their sin. Through the law with its sacrifices, he made a way for their sins to be covered, picturing the coming of the Savior who would one day take away their sin forever. All he desired was their love and obedience, and to be glorified through them as their good and merciful Father; but they were not willing to glorify him as God.

Instead of seeing these sacrifices as a picture of God's love, and worshipping him because of it, they elevated the laws in importance. They did not see in the law, the sinfulness of their sin and need for a Savior, but rather a license to sin. The performance of these sacrifices became the measure of righteousness for them instead of genuinely repenting of their sin and living by faith. They did not seek to become godlier or glorifying to God, but only to clear their consciences when they were not.

I remember as a teenager growing up in the Catholic church, my best friend and I, in our own self-righteousness, would attend Saturday evening mass together. We would go to confession and perform our penance in anticipation of the sins we were planning to commit that night, as a sort of *indulgence*, I suppose. Performing these works established (at least in our own minds) our righteousness, but obviously did not attain to the righteousness of God which is by faith.

We did not seek to live by faith, attempting to obey his commands, but went as far against them as we thought we could get away with. Our religion was not worship. It was pretense. As a matter of fact, we went through these motions over and over, week after week, with no thought of genuine repentance toward God. We were so intent on fulfilling the laws of the Catholic Church, that we did not even consider trying to please God.

We, like the Pharisees, even came up with additional rules with which to further establish our righteousness. We kissed the crucifix necklaces we wore and made the sign of the cross each time we passed a Catholic Church. We even reproved others for their lack of attendance to church. How proud we were of the sacrifices we offered to God. We were basically Catholic Pharisees. No wonder Jesus called them hypocrites.

> "And he said unto them, Full well ye reject the commandment of God, that ye may keep your own

tradition." (Mark 7:9)

I believe this is a picture of what the law had become for the Jews. They gave to God, not their love and worship and certainly not their obedience, but only what was required by the law. They were not truly worshipping God, but going through the motions of serving him, while in truth they were serving only themselves.

> "...this people draw near me with their mouth, and with their lips do honour me, but have removed their heart far from me, and their fear toward me is taught by the precept of men:" (Isaiah 29:13)

Their hearts were far from God and their fear toward him was taught only by the precept of men, as were mine and my friend's. This was not faith in God, and he was certainly not pleased. As a matter of fact, he was sickened, and rightfully so. Because of Israel's refusal to turn to God with their whole heart, God blinded them to the truth of Christ. What was needed was a genuine turning to God. He did not desire their empty works or their words, but their hearts.

> "If thou shalt hearken unto the voice of the LORD thy God, to keep his commandments and his statutes which are written in this book of the law, and if thou turn unto the LORD thy God with all thine heart, and with all thy soul." (Deuteronomy 30:10)

It is still the same for us today. God does not desire our lip-service or our religion, but our hearts. Our religion sickens him without a heart that is genuinely seeking to please him. Thinking that we can be reconciled to God through a prayer while our hearts remain far from him in disobedience and sin is no less hypocrisy than going through the motions of the law.

> "I hate, I despise your feast days, and I will not smell in your solemn assemblies. Though ye offer me burnt offerings and your meat offerings, I will not accept them: neither will I regard the peace offerings of your fat beasts. Take thou away from me the noise of thy songs; for I will not hear the melody of thy viols. But let judgment run down as waters, and righteousness as a mighty stream. Have ye offered unto me sacrifices and offerings in the wilderness forty years, O house of Israel. But ye have borne the tabernacle of your Moloch and Chiun your images, the star of your god, which ye made to yourselves." (Amos 5:21-26)

Why did God hate their sacrifices? Because of their hypocrisy. God abhorred the Israelites' attempts to satisfy him with their sacrifices and their feasts and festivals offered in his name while they continued in their disobedience and worshipping of other gods.

They offered to him sacrifices only to appease him rather than giving him their hearts. This false worship was not a sweet-smelling savor unto him, but a stench in his nostrils that he would not accept. He would not hear their songs or receive their sacrifices, while they cleaved to their sins.

We see this over and over throughout the Bible. It is our hearts that God wants, not our professions or our religion that praises him with our lips while our hearts are far from him. God tells us that "…to obey is better than sacrifice… (1Samuel 15:22)

Many unbelievers claim to seek the wisdom of God or petition him through prayers in a moment of desperation; but without a genuine turning to him they will not receive that which they seek after. As we see in Ezekiel, those who approach God through pretense or hypocrisy (believers or unbelievers) are answered according to their hypocrisy.

"Son of man, these men have set up their idols in their heart, and put the stumblingblock of their iniquity before their face: should I be enquired of at all by them? Therefore speak unto them, and say unto them, Thus saith the Lord GOD; Every man of the house of Israel that **setteth up his idols in his heart, and putteth the stumblingblock of his iniquity before his face**, and cometh to the prophet; **I the LORD will answer him that cometh according to the multitude of his idols**; That I may take the house of Israel in their own heart, because they are all estranged from me through their idols. Therefore say unto the house of Israel, Thus saith the Lord GOD; Repent, and turn yourselves from your idols; and turn away your faces from all your abominations." (Ezekiel 14:3-6)

This is the same thing many do today, adding God as merely *another god in* their lives, and not as the God *of* their lives. We cannot approach God with the stumbling block of our iniquity before our faces while we embrace idols such as sports, TV, money, family, pets, relationships, and careers that we have set up in our hearts. Whatever it is that we love the most, that's first in our hearts, *is* our god and most often rules our lives. God will not be second. He demands to be *the* God of our lives alone. Unless we are willing to repent and believe in him *as our only God,* we cannot come to him.

"But **without faith it is impossible** to please him: for **he that cometh to God must believe that he is**, and that he is a rewarder of them that diligently seek him." (Hebrews 11:6)

We must turn from our sin toward him *as* God. This repentance toward God is essential if we are to receive the sacrifice he has provided. Let me assure you, this is not Lordship salvation, but biblical salvation.

To believe in God means a great deal more than merely acknowledging his existence, or even going through the motions of religion. Just knowing that he is God is not enough.

> "For the invisible things of him from the creation of the world are clearly seen, being understood by the things that are made, even his eternal power and Godhead; so that they are without excuse: Because that, **when they knew God, they glorified him not as God,** neither were thankful; but became vain in their imaginations, and their foolish heart was darkened." (Romans 1:20-21)

The problem was not a lack of knowledge of God, but that those who knew God were not willing to turn to him and glorify him *as* God, much like the Agnostics today. The Agnostics won't deny that there *is* a God but refuse any knowledge that he has given to reveal himself to man, rejecting his authority as if to say, "He may be God; but he's not my God." They will not be told what to do by him.

This is nothing new. It was the same with Pharaoh. Although the heavens declare the glory of God, Pharaoh also would not hear, and denied knowledge of God, refusing to obey him.

> "And Pharaoh said, Who is the LORD, that I should obey his voice to let Israel go? I know not the LORD, neither will I let Israel go." (Exodus 5:2)

I find it interesting that studies have shown Atheists and Agnostics seventy six percent more willing to believe in extra-terrestrials than Christians are. Apparently, they can accept the idea that there are supernatural beings with superior knowledge, existing possibly outside of time, that have supposedly visited earth and have secretly intervened in the lives of men throughout history, as long as they are aliens and not God. Although there is no physical proof of such alien beings, this explanation of the supernatural is somehow more acceptable to them than God.

Why? Could it be because aliens (at least so far) have not condemned man's sins or demanded their obedience? Aliens are not demanding to be *their* god. Clearly, Atheists and Agnostics have a desire to believe in something, but they *choose not* to believe in God.

To believe in God, means to believe that he is God with all the power and authority of God, deserving of our worship, and believing that he is the rewarder of them that diligently seek him. Without that willingness to glorify him as God, as we are told in Romans chapter one, they became vain in their imaginations and their foolish hearts were darkened. As we read further, we see that because of this, they were led into idolatry and wicked immorality instead of salvation.

Many people suggest that if man sincerely worships in *some* way, that it should be pleasing to God, that God should see their desire to worship him and accept *any* form of religion or idol worship, even if it is in error. They insist that if man's heart is right, no matter how much in error his religion may be, God will accept it.

The problem is that idolatry and false religion are proof that man's heart is not right. Idolatry is the direct result of the rejection of God.

When man refuses to yield to the God who demands obedience and repentance from sin, his inward knowledge of the existence of God and his natural desire to worship *something* causes him to invent for himself another god. He makes for himself one which he *can* accept- one that does not infringe upon his lifestyle, or demand change.

He refuses to humble himself before the holy and righteous God of the universe; so, he creates gods of wood or stone, or carved images, some in the forms of natural man, or even woman. Others create for themselves an imaginary version of God suited to their own desires. This God accepts and understands their immorality, addictions and worldly desires.

In this way, man minimizes *his new god*, bringing him down to his own level, thereby minimizing the conviction of sin. These imaginary gods demand only that which they desire to give, good deeds, charity, or contributions to causes and campaigns. By these they justify themselves and maintain their own pride and self-sufficiency, while allowing themselves to remain in sin.

Sometimes they even bargain with these gods, trading these worthless offerings in attempts to pay for their sins; but without the shedding of blood, there is no forgiveness of sins. (Hebrews 9:22)

God cannot accept the worship of anyone or anything other than himself. True worship is the recognition of God's righteous rule and reign over his own creation. It demands a recognition of sins and acceptance by faith of God's prescribed plan of salvation through the shed blood of his Son, Jesus Christ. All other offerings are only filthy and worthless in his sight. If we are to be saved, we must be willing to repent and turn to him *as our* God.

The question is *who* will be God in our lives?

For Eve, the choice was clear. She wanted to be as God, so that she could be her own God. It was the same for Cain. Although he offered sacrifices to God much the same as Abel; he chose to decide *what* he would offer, rather than submitting to God's authority. He was choosing to be his own god.

The apostle Paul called for the unbelievers in Athens to turn from their idols to God. He preached to them who God was and how he was to be worshipped warning them that he had appointed a day when the world would be judged for their sins by his Son, Jesus Christ.

This essential need for submission to God's authority is illustrated throughout the Bible.

In chapters three and four of the New Testament book of Hebrews, we're reminded of the wilderness wanderings of the Israelites. If you remember, Moses, by the power of God, led the Israelites out of Egypt. Although God showed himself as God, full of power and glory through many miracles, even going before them; the Israelites grumbled and complained, desiring instead to return to the bondage of Egypt.

When it came time to enter the promised land, Moses sent twelve men (one from every tribe of Israel, everyone a ruler among them) to spy out the land of Canaan. When they returned, ten gave an evil report, claiming that they could not stand before the inhabitants there.

Although God had told them that he had given them the land and not to fear, they feared exceedingly and refused to obey God. They, through their testimony caused all of Israel to grumble and fear even wishing they had died in the wilderness rather than going on to the promised land.

These, who had before appeared to believe, even following Moses into the wilderness, failed the test of faith, their disobedience proving their unbelief. These chose to turn from God and leaned instead to their own understanding.

Only two, Joshua and Caleb believed that God was able to fulfil his promise and deliver them safely. Those who refused to obey God did not receive the promise. Instead, God made them wander in the wilderness for another forty years until that generation passed away in the wilderness, as they had wished.

"And the LORD'S anger was kindled against Israel,

and he made them wander in the wilderness forty years, until all the generation, that had done evil in the sight of the LORD, was consumed." (Numbers 32:13)

Because of their unbelief, an entire generation could not enter into God's rest. They did not believe that God was God and was able to deliver them safely. Their disobedience proved their unbelief.

"And to whom sware he that they should not enter into his rest, but to them that believed not? So we see that they could not enter in because of unbelief." (Hebrews 3:18-19)

They could not cease from their long and difficult journey and receive the glorious blessings God had promised, but were made to continue wandering, until they died.

In Hebrews chapter three, the writer exhorts us:

"Wherefore (as the Holy Ghost saith, To day if ye will hear his voice, Harden not your hearts, as in the provocation, in the day of temptation in the wilderness:" (Hebrews 3:7-8)

Because the offer of rest is still promised to us through salvation in Jesus Christ, we are warned not to harden our hearts and follow the same pattern of unbelief.

"Let us therefore fear, lest, a promise being left us of entering into his rest, any of you should seem to come short of it." (Hebrews 4:1)

Disobedience is evidence of unbelief. Those who claim to love God but refuse to obey him are, according to

Scripture, liars and the truth is not in them.

> "He that saith, I know him, and keepeth not his commandments, is a liar, and the truth is not in him." (1 John 2:4)

Yet today, we regularly invite those who live as though there is no God, to enter into his rest in return for a sinner's prayer. Those who claim to believe in God, yet have no desire to glorify him *as* God, are urged to come and partake of God's rest in Christ if they will just pray a prayer.

Modern Christianity has even redefined repentance as a turning from *unbelief in Christ* to *belief in Christ*, rather than a turning from sin to God. Some of these even suggest that John's call for repentance was only a change of mind to belief in Christ. That simply does not agree with Scripture.

> "Bring forth therefore fruits worthy of repentance..." (Luke 3:8)

> "And the people asked him, [John] saying, What shall we do then? He answereth and saith unto them, He that hath two coats, let him impart to him that hath none; and he that hath meat, let him do likewise. **Then came also publicans to be baptized, and said unto him, Master, what shall we do? And he said unto them, Exact no more than that which is appointed you. And the soldiers likewise demanded of him, saying, And what shall we do? And he said unto them, Do violence to no man, neither accuse any falsely; and be content with your wages.**" (Luke 3:10-14)

Clearly, John called for repentance from sin in preparation to receive Christ. Remember, Paul preached that repentance is toward God, and faith toward Christ. I'm sure that some of you are thinking that as long as our converts believe in Jesus, then there should be no problem. I would ask then, how *can* they truly believe in Christ (God with us) if they will not repent of their sin toward God and believe in him *as* God?

Can a rebellious sinner who refuses to obey God, even possibly comprehend the need for the salvation he is offering if they are unwilling to consider their need to be right with God? Unless they believe that God has the rightful authority to judge them and to condemn them for their sin, what condemnation can they be saved from? According to Jesus, only those who see and understand their need to be made right before God, can see their need for Christ.

> "When Jesus heard it, he saith unto them, They that are whole have no need of the physician, but they that are sick: I came not to call the righteous, but sinners to repentance." (Mark 2:17)

Jesus is God in the flesh. The same things that the Father hates, Jesus hates. Can an idolatrous sinner continue in his rejection of God and think he can be reconciled to him through Jesus? Certainly, Jesus would no more accept this than the Father.

Modern Christianity, however, invites these rebellious sinners who, like the Israelites, are not willing to believe God's promises or turn to him in repentance, to enter into his rest. How did God view this type of unbelief? If you remember, Israel's refusal to believe and obey provoked him to wrath.

> "So I sware in my wrath, They shall not enter into my rest.)" (Hebrews 3:11)

God did not welcome them. He angrily refused them.

God does not offer deliverance or rest to those who will not first believe in him. What rest can there be for sinners today if they have not been willing to look to God?

Jesus himself says, "Come unto me, all ye that labour and are heavy laden, and I will give you rest." "For my yoke is easy, and my burden is light." (Matthew 11:28 & 30)

What labor is Christ referring to? The labor of the works of the law, by which men sought to be made right with God. Salvation in Christ offers rest from these works and from the burden of sin for those who will believe in him. Clearly, there is an assumption of a desire to be right with God and an understanding of sin.

> "...for he that cometh to God must believe that he is, and that he is a rewarder of them that diligently seek him." (Hebrews 11:6)

When God commanded Abraham to offer his son Isaac as a sacrifice, Abraham's obedience showed his belief that God was able to raise him up again and to keep his promises. He believed that God was God and a rewarder of them that diligently seek him.

In God's provision of the ram as a substitutionary sacrifice, it's easy to see Christ as *our* sacrifice; but what we also need to see is that it was only after Abraham lifted the knife demonstrating his obedience, that the ram was seen. The proof of Abraham's belief in God preceded the revelation of the substitutionary sacrifice God provided. Notice the pattern: willingness to submit to God's authority, then deliverance.

-Noah also showed his belief by obeying God to the building of the ark. Because of his belief, he and his family were saved from the flood.

-Moses obeyed God, and led the children of Israel out of Egypt.

-Joshua and Caleb obeyed God and entered the promised land.

Now, before you write these off as merely Old Testament scenarios under a different economy, or simply blessings of obedient believers, remember that John the Baptist also came preaching repentance toward God.

> "And he shall go before him in the spirit and power of Elias, **to turn the hearts of the fathers to the children, and the disobedient to the wisdom of the just; to make ready a people prepared for the Lord.**" (Luke 1:17)

John preached repentance from sin, not only for obedience to the law, but in preparation for belief in the one who would come after him, to make ready a people prepared for the Lord Jesus Christ.

Please do not misunderstand. I am not suggesting that a man must perform works or demonstrate a certain number of efforts toward obedience before faith in Christ is possible. Works do not save. These are only evidences of willingness to turn to God in repentance and glorify him *as* God, showing a heart that is tender toward God. This willingness to believe God is the heart of repentance.

Repentance, like works, does not save. It is not reconciliation; it merely shows the *desire* for reconciliation, the necessary preparation of the heart to receive faith in Christ. Repentance merely softens the heart to allow the seed of faith to penetrate. The Bible is clear that as New Testament believers we can only be reconciled to God through faith in Christ.

> "Jesus saith unto him, I am the way, the truth, and the life: no man cometh unto the Father, but by me." (John 14:6)

The modern gospel message of *just accept Jesus* attempts to go around God to Jesus. We cannot come to Christ without first recognizing our condemnation before God.

He that is not willing to obey God shows his unbelief in God. When Paul was imprisoned. He believed in God's provision and reward, and accepted his fate, even singing hymns in the night. He believed God and praised him, and God delivered him. Belief in God must come before deliverance.

> "If I regard iniquity in my heart, the Lord will not hear me:" (Psalms 66:18)

> "Salvation is far from the wicked: for they seek not thy statutes." (Psalms 119:155)

We are not called to preach a message of *just accept Christ*. The message committed to us is this: "be ye reconciled to God."

> "**Now then we are ambassadors for Christ**, as though God did beseech you by us: **we pray you in Christ's stead, be ye reconciled to God.**" (2 Corinthians 5:20)

Be ye reconciled to God! This statement suggests the very necessary questions that the lost should be contemplating.

"Who is this God that I should be reconciled to him?"
"Am I separated from God? I thought I was ok."
"What is it that separates me from God?"
"How can I be reconciled to God?"

When Paul stood on Mars hill speaking to the men of Athens, he did not merely call them to *accept Jesus*. He called for them to turn from their idols to God. These, who were overcome in idolatry, were worshipping an image made unto "the unknown god". Paul preached to them their need to turn to the living God, and he declared to them who he is.

"That they should seek the Lord, if haply they might feel after him, and find him, though he be not far from every one of us: For in him we live, and move, and have our being; as certain also of your own poets have said, For we are also his offspring. Forasmuch then as we are the offspring of God, we ought not to think that the Godhead is like unto gold, or silver, or stone, graven by art and man's device. And the times of this ignorance God winked at; **but now commandeth all men every where to repent:**" (Acts 17:27-30)

Paul was not commanding them to turn from their unbelief in Christ to belief in Christ, but to turn from their idolatry, to the living God, in order to be reconciled to him through Christ. It was their unbelief in God *as their* God that was the problem.

"Because he hath appointed a day, in the which he will judge the world in righteousness by that man whom he hath ordained; whereof he hath given assurance unto all men, in that he hath raised him from the dead." (Acts 17:31)

When John the Baptist called for repentance, we are told that those being baptized came confessing their sins. We are all aware of the great commission and willing to accept our responsibility to the lost; but what exactly are we to be preaching? Jesus himself called for the preaching of *repentance and remission of sins* to all the earth.

> "And that **repentance and remission of sins** should be preached in his name among all nations, beginning at Jerusalem." (Luke 24:47)

Christ himself was obedient to the Father even unto death. He is our example in all things.

> "I can of mine own self do nothing: as I hear, I judge: and my judgment is just; because I seek not mine own will, but the will of the Father which hath sent me." (John 5:30)

Everything he did was to please God- to the glory of God.

> "That all men should honour the Son, even as they honour the Father. He that honoureth not the Son honoureth not the Father ...." (John 5:23)

Somehow, we seem to have forgotten that God's plan of salvation has always been to reconcile sinful man to himself.

God's plan of salvation was not just to save man from condemnation, or even to glorify Jesus. If those were God's only desires, he could have simply sent Christ immediately after the fall. We see though that God went to great lengths to show himself and to draw men to himself, for his own glory. God's plan was to glorify himself. He called out the people of Israel, making them his people who would represent him to the entire world.

> "And what one nation in the earth is like thy people, even like Israel, whom God went to redeem for a people to himself, and to make him a name, and to do for you great things and terrible, for thy land, before thy

people, which thou redeemedst to thee from Egypt, from the nations and their gods?" (2 Samuel 7:23)

These were to be an example to all, of God's goodness and mercy as well as his fierce judgment. He promised them blessings and fruitfulness for their obedience and punishment and cursing for their disobedience (which showed their unbelief).

"I call heaven and earth to record this day against you, that I have set before you life and death, blessing and cursing: therefore choose life, that both thou and thy seed may live:" (Deuteronomy 30:19)

Those who wished to receive God's blessings and escape God's curses, showed their faith by obedience to the law. In the sacrifices of the law were constant reminders of sin and the need for repentance and atonement of sins. The blood sacrifices pictured a life given for the life of a sinner. The purpose of course was to keep the heart tender to the cost of sin and toward God.

If all man had to do was *accept Jesus*, then why would God have given the law? God's word declares that the law was the schoolmaster to lead us to Christ, and that by the law *is the knowledge of sin,* which separates us from God. Clearly, God gave us the law to show us *our sin against him* and *the need to be reconciled through a Savior*. It is only through *trying and failing* to please God through our obedience that we see how wicked we truly are. Sin becomes more sinful and our condemnation just, proving our need for a Savior.

Adam and Eve knew that there was a God. They walked and talked with him every day. Yet they refused to obey him. Eve was deceived into questioning the truth of God's word. She trusted in the serpent's word rather than God's word; but Adam was not deceived. It was Adam's *willing* disobedience that removed them from their place of blessing and brought cursing instead.

> "For as by one man's **disobedience** many were made sinners, so by the obedience of one shall many be made righteous." (Romans 5:19)

God desires to be our God, with all the authority that comes with that title, to his own glory. Yet we disregard this vital truth and push for faith in Christ without repentance toward God to those with little or no regard for God.

These have no investment in the sacrifice of Christ, because they have no awareness of the cost of sin. That is why the preaching of the cross is only foolishness to them. The modern gospel tells them to just turn from their unbelief in Christ to belief in Christ, but they have no need to believe in him.

If they will not believe the Father, how can they receive the Son? It is our sin and rebellion against God that separates us from God, and that is what must be repented of. Because of Israel's refusal to hear and obey God, all but the elect, were blinded to the gospel.

> "What then? Israel hath not obtained that which he seeketh for; **but the election hath obtained it**, and the rest were blinded (According as it is written, God hath given them the spirit of slumber, eyes that they should not see, and ears that they should not hear;) unto this day." (Romans 11:7-8)

Who were the elect? Were they just a random group chosen for salvation while the rest were chosen for damnation? No, they were the few who *did obey God* and hearken to his word -a faithful *believing* remnant that did desire righteousness.

In Romans chapter eleven, Paul, speaking of them reminds us of Elijah. When Elijah stood against the prophets of Baal, proving that God was the only true God, Jezebel sought to kill him. Elijah, in discouragement cried out to God saying, "because the children of Israel have forsaken thy covenant, thrown down thine altars, and slain thy prophets with the sword; and I, even I only, am left; "(1 Kings 19:14)

Although it appeared to Elijah that all of Israel had forsaken the Lord, God told him that was not so. He told Elijah that he had seven thousand more left in Israel. Who were these seven thousand? We read that they were those who had not forsaken God, who, "…have not bowed unto Baal, and every mouth which hath not kissed him." (1Kings 19:18)

In every generation there is *a faithful remnant* of true believers.

> "And the dragon was wroth with the woman, and went to make war with the remnant of her seed, **which keep the commandments of God, and have the testimony of Jesus Christ**." (Revelation 12:17)

Even during the great tribulation, we see that there will be a faithful remnant. The elect spoken of in Romans who were saved according to the election of grace, were the faithful believers in God, who had come to him through Christ to be regenerated by the Holy Spirit. The rest, those who would not obey were blinded to salvation by grace and would continue seeking their own righteousness through the law.

Those who *would not obey* God *could not see* salvation in Jesus. Why do we think it should be different for us now?

"In whom **the god of this world hath blinded the minds of them which believe not**, lest the light of the glorious gospel of Christ, who is the image of God, should shine unto them." (2 Corinthians 4:4)

Those who will not repent and believe in God are *blinded to the gospel* of Christ just the same as Israel. The only difference is that these are not blinded as a result of God's judgement, but *by their own sin and rejection of God*. A heart that is hardened in sin is hardened *against* the truth.

> "**Evil men understand not judgment**: but they that seek the LORD understand all things." (Proverbs 28:5)

> "As it is written in the law of Moses, all this evil is come upon us: yet made we not our prayer before the LORD our God, **that we might turn from our iniquities, and understand thy truth.**" (Daniel 9:13)

Preaching a gospel message that does not include repentance often results in false professions from those still blinded by sin. I believe that this is the reason we are currently witnessing an entire generation of professing Christians, who like the Israelites, refuse to obey God.

These Christians live as though there is no God, demanding the liberty to live like the world rather than Christ. They walk and talk and act like the world, even loving the world; and although they do not appear to love God, they claim the name of Christ.

> "Know ye not that the unrighteous shall not inherit the kingdom of God? **Be not deceived: neither fornicators, nor idolaters, nor adulterers, nor effeminate, nor abusers of themselves with mankind, Nor thieves, nor covetous, nor drunkards, nor revilers, nor extortioners, shall inherit the kingdom of God.**" (1 Corinthians 6:9-10)

"Now the works of the flesh are manifest, which are these; Adultery, fornication, uncleanness, lasciviousness, Idolatry, witchcraft, hatred, variance, emulations, wrath, strife, seditions, heresies, Envyings, murders, drunkenness, revellings, and such like: of the which I tell you before, as I have also told you in time past, that **they which do such things shall not inherit the kingdom of God.**" (Galatians 5:19-21)

Someday they will stand before the Lord and hear, "…I never knew you: depart from me, ye that work iniquity." (Matthew 7:23) Woe to us if we are responsible for their destruction rather than their salvation!

CHAPTER 3
THE HEARING OF FAITH

Someone asked me recently, "If we don't lead people through a prayer, then how do they get saved?" I told them, "the same way they did in the Bible."

When Cornelius, a Gentile who believed God, prayed, God came to him in a vision telling him to send for Peter who would tell him *words whereby* he would be saved (the gospel).

> "And he shewed us how he had seen an angel in his house, which stood and said unto him, Send men to Joppa, and call for Simon, whose surname is Peter; **Who shall tell thee words, whereby thou and all thy house shall be saved**." (Acts 11:13-14)

> "**While Peter yet spake** these words, the Holy Ghost fell on all them which heard the word. (Acts 10:44)

Notice, that it was *while Peter was still speaking the words of life* that they received the Holy Spirit of Christ. They were regenerated by the Holy Spirit without uttering a single word of their own.

> "Can any man forbid water, that these should not be baptized, **which have received the Holy Ghost as well as we?**" (Acts 10:4)

They were saved by the hearing of faith.

In Acts, chapter fifteen, Peter recounts this event.

"And when there had been much disputing, Peter rose up, and said unto them, Men and brethren, ye know how that a good while ago God made choice among us, **that the Gentiles by my mouth should hear the word of the gospel, and believe.** And **God, which knoweth the hearts, bare them witness, giving them the Holy Ghost**, even as he did unto us;" (Acts 15:7-8)

He told the hearers that the Gentiles heard the gospel, believed, and then God, who knew their hearts, witnessed of their faith by giving them the gift of the Holy Spirit. Not one place is a prayer, or a decision even suggested. They did not verbally call upon God and ask for salvation. The fact that they were there and willing to hear suggests that like Cornelius, these were already believers in God who desired salvation, but the receiving of it was by faith, not by a prayer.

According to the Bible, we are saved through hearing the words of life preached, coming to a knowledge of the truth, and through believing, we are saved. Then we confess that salvation.

When we read the account of Philip witnessing to the Ethiopian Eunuch, we see that the Eunuch was anxious to be baptized as a public association with Christ. He asked Philip, "...See, here is water; what doth hinder me to be baptized?" (Acts 8:36). Philip's answer was not, "you must say a prayer first, or verbally confess Jesus." Instead, he said, "if thou believest with all thine heart, thou mayest..." (Acts 8:37)

Since we know that baptism is for those who are saved, we can easily see that Phillip was establishing that belief is the instrument through which salvation is received, not speaking the words of a prayer.

On the day of Pentecost, as Peter preached, we are told that those that heard him "were pricked in their heart, and said unto Peter and to the rest of the apostles, Men and brethren, what shall we do?" (Acts 2:37)

Again, we see that Peter did not lead them through a

sinner's prayer but told them:

> "Repent, and be baptized every one of you in the name of Jesus Christ for the remission of sins, and ye shall receive the gift of the Holy Ghost." (Acts 2:38)

We read then that they that believed were baptized and joined themselves to the church, "And they continued steadfastly in the apostles' doctrine and fellowship, and in breaking of bread, and in prayers." (Acts 2:42) That doesn't sound much like our converts today, does it?

Our job is to go and preach, admonishing those who believe to publicly testify of their faith through believer's baptism and to join themselves to the church. Then we are to teach them, so that they can go and do the same.

It is not our responsibility to pronounce sinners saved or to seal the deal with a prayer. Only the Holy Spirit of God can seal their salvation. We cannot direct or initiate salvation for anyone. We simply do not have the power within ourselves. Only the Holy Spirit of God can do that. Only God can save.

> "It is the spirit that quickeneth; the flesh profiteth nothing: **the words that I speak unto you, they are spirit, and they are life.**" (John 6:63)

Jesus Christ *is* the living Word of God- the very Word of life. He is light and life and it is his word that shines the glorious gospel into the hearts of men, bringing them out of darkness and into the light of new life. It is the Word of God, the *Word of life*, that imparts the truth of the gospel, bringing us to faith, and it is that faith that saves us.

> "In the beginning was the Word, and the Word was with God, and the Word was God. The same was in the beginning with God. All things were made by him; and without him was not any thing made that was made.

In him was life; and the life was the light of men." (John 1:1-4)

"That which was from the beginning, which we have heard, which we have seen with our eyes, which we have looked upon, and our hands have handled, of the Word of life;" (1 John 1:1)

"Then Simon Peter answered him, Lord, to whom shall we go? thou hast the words of eternal life." (John 6:68)

Sadly somehow, we have come to the place in our Christianity that we no longer trust the words of life to save sinners. Instead, we apply our own humanistic ideas, attempting to initiate salvation by a prayer, as though we can direct the Holy Spirit by our own command.

How easily we forget that "The wind bloweth where it listeth, and thou hearest the sound thereof, but canst not tell whence it cometh, and whither it goeth: so is every one that is born of the Spirit." (John 3:8)

We praise God's word and claim to revere it. We readily believe that God had the power to *speak the world into existence by his word*, yet we doubt its power to save. It is that same power of the word that created the world that also creates new life.

"Being **born again, not of corruptible seed**, but of incorruptible, **by the word of God**, which liveth and abideth for ever." (1 Peter 1:23)

It is by the power of God's word (the incorruptible seed), that we are saved and yet, when it comes to evangelism, we lean to our own understanding. We have simply refused the power of his word in salvation. Even Bible believing Christians who heartily reject the false doctrine of a works-based salvation, regularly subvert the power of God's word, *substituting the words of man* as the catalyst for salvation instead. How dare we? If this is not a doctrine of devils, I don't know what is.

Salvation has always, only been by grace, through the instrument of faith. The fruits of this false doctrine speak for themselves. When we seal salvations with the Sinner's Prayer rather than the Holy Spirit of God, making salvations by confession, is it any wonder we have an epidemic of *Lord, Lord* conversions?

We have created a false doctrine of receiving Christ by a prayer, based on our misinterpretation of Romans chapter ten, despite the multitudes of Scriptures that tell us that we are saved by believing.

> "And Crispus, the chief ruler of the synagogue, believed on the Lord with all his house; and many of the Corinthians **hearing believed, and were baptized**." (Acts 18:8)

> "But we are not of them who draw back unto perdition; **but of them that believe to the saving of the soul**." (Hebrews 10:39)

> "And brought them out, and said, Sirs, **what must I do to be saved? And they said, Believe on the Lord Jesus Christ, and thou shalt be saved**, and thy house." (Acts 16:30-31)

> "That **whosoever believeth in him** should not perish, but have eternal life." (John 3:15)

> "For God so loved the world, that he gave his only begotten Son, that **whosoever believeth in him** should not perish, but have everlasting life." (John 3:16)

> "**He that believeth on him** is not condemned: but he that believeth not is condemned already, because he hath not believed in the name of the only begotten Son

of God." (John 3:18)

"**He that believeth on the Son** hath everlasting life: and he that believeth not the Son shall not see life; but the wrath of God abideth on him." (John 3:36)

"Verily, verily, I say unto you, He that **heareth my word, and believeth on him that sent me**, hath everlasting life, and shall not come into condemnation; but is passed from death unto life." (John 5:24)

"And Jesus said unto them, I am the bread of life: he that cometh to me shall never hunger; and **he that believeth on me** shall never thirst." (John 6:35)

"And this is the will of him that sent me, that every one which seeth the Son, and **believeth on him**, may have everlasting life: and I will raise him up at the last day." (John 6:40)

"**He that believeth on me**, as the Scripture hath said, out of his belly shall flow rivers of living water." (John 7:38)

"Jesus said unto her, I am the resurrection, and the life: **he that believeth in** me, though he were dead, yet shall he live. And whosoever liveth and believeth in me shall never die. Believest thou this?" (John 11:25-26)

"Verily, verily, I say unto you, **He that believeth on me**, the works that I do shall he do also; and greater works than these shall he do; because I go unto my Father." (John 14:12)

"To him give all the prophets witness, that through his name **whosoever believeth in him** shall receive remission of sins." (Acts 10:43)

"For I am not ashamed of the gospel of Christ: for it is the power of God unto salvation to **every one that believeth**; to the Jew first, and also to the Greek." (Romans 1:16)

"To declare, I say, at this time his righteousness: that he might be just, and the justifier of him which **believeth in Jesus.**" (Romans 3:26)

"But to him that worketh not, **but believeth on him** that justifieth the ungodly, his faith is counted for righteousness." (Romans 4:5)

"As it is written, Behold, I lay in Sion a stumblingstone and rock of offence: and **whosoever believeth on hi**m shall not be ashamed." (Romans 9:33)

"For Christ is the end of the law for righteousness to **every one that believeth.**" (Romans 10:4)

"Wherefore also it is contained in the Scripture, Behold, I lay in Sion a chief corner stone, elect, precious: and **he that believeth on him** shall not be confounded." (1 Peter 2:6)

"Who is he that overcometh the world, but **he that believeth that Jesus is the Son of God?**" (1 John 5:5)

"**He that believeth on the Son of God** hath the witness in himself: he that believeth not God hath made him a liar; because he believeth not the record that God gave of his Son." (1 John 5:10)

The list could go on and on, showing that we are saved by the hearing of faith, not by deciding or praying. Now, before you decide that I'm leaning toward Calvinism, let me assure you that I am not. I am not suggesting that God saves us against our will or apart from any decision of our own.

While salvation is totally of God, we do have a free will and the ability to reject God's offer of salvation. The issue is, where exactly does our decision come in? The Bible tells us over and over that it is our responsibility to hear or to hearken to the word of God.

> "If any man have ears to hear, let him hear. And he said unto them, Take heed what ye hear: with what measure ye mete, it shall be measured to you: and unto you that hear shall more be given." (Mark 4:23-24)

From the garden, man's responsibility was to hearken to God's command. God gave him a choice to obey and enjoy the manifold blessings God had provided or disobey and receive punishment. There was only one command given, not to eat of the tree of knowledge of good and evil. Adam, however, chose to hearken to the voice of his wife instead.

> "And unto Adam he said, Because thou hast hearkened unto the voice of thy wife, and hast eaten of the tree, of which I commanded thee, saying, Thou shalt not eat of it: cursed is the ground for thy sake; in sorrow shalt thou eat of it all the days of thy life;" (Genesis 3:17)

By his disobedience, sin entered into the world, and death passed upon all men. Man has always had a choice.

> "For as by one man's disobedience many were made sinners, so by the obedience of one shall many be made righteous." (Romans 5:19)

As we have already seen, according to Romans chapter one, the knowledge of God is available to all, because God has shown it to all. With this knowledge of God comes a choice.

> "For the invisible things of him from the creation

of the world are clearly seen, being understood by the things that are made, even his eternal power and Godhead; so that they are without excuse: Because that, when they knew God, they glorified him not as God, neither were thankful; but became vain in their imaginations, and their foolish heart was darkened:" (Romans 1:20-21)

We can either choose to glorify him *as* God, or we can refuse and harden our hearts against him, willingly blinding ourselves to the truth. The word of God cannot produce saving faith in a heart that is hardened in sin and rebellion against God. This is beautifully illustrated in the parable of the sower:

"And he spake many things unto them in parables, saying, Behold, a sower went forth to sow; And when he sowed, some seeds fell by the way side, and the fowls came and devoured them up: Some fell upon stony places, where they had not much earth: and forthwith they sprung up, because they had no deepness of earth: And when the sun was up, they were scorched; and because they had no root, they withered away. And some fell among thorns; and the thorns sprung up, and choked them: But other fell into good ground, and brought forth fruit, some an hundredfold, some sixtyfold, some thirtyfold. Who hath ears to hear, let him hear." (Matthew 13:3-9)

This parable illustrates different responses to the gospel message and how the condition of our heart effects the reception of the word.

Now, before we can understand the truths in this passage, it is essential that we define the terms used.

1. The sower is Jesus (or now, Jesus in us)
2. The seed is the word of God, the gospel (the

incorruptible seed by which we are born again)
    3.   The field is the world (the unsaved)
    4.   The soil is the heart (of the unsaved)
    5.   The fruit produced by the incorruptible seed of the word is saving faith.

The last point is where many become confused. It is vitally important to remember that the seed of the word, sown into the good soil of a heart produces as its fruit, saving faith *not* good works.

> "Hear ye therefore the parable of the sower. When any one heareth the word of the kingdom, and understandeth it not, then cometh the wicked one, and catcheth away that which was sown in his heart. This is he which received seed by the wayside." (Matthew 13:18-19)

The wayside is a description of a traveled road or path. In farming, it would be the path the farmer walked on to throw seed onto the field. As he walked, he would pack down the soil under his feet, hardening it with every step.

This ground would not easily receive seed or allow it to take root and grow into faith. The seed would be trodden under foot or remain on top of the hard ground for the birds to come and steal away.

In the parallel passage in Luke, we read that they had not yet believed or been saved.

> "Those by the way side are they that hear; then cometh the devil, and taketh away the word out of their hearts, **lest they should believe and be saved.**" (Luke 8:12)

We can easily see that the fruit expected from the sowing of the word is saving faith because the taking away of the seed was to prevent them from believing and being saved.

Those who received the seed by the wayside had hearts that were still too hardened for the gospel to penetrate. The seed of the word did not take root and produce saving faith. What was it that hardened their hearts? Sin. Only repentance toward God can break through that hard soil.

Trying to lead someone through a sinner's prayer before the Devil steals it away, as some suggest, would do them no good if the word, as we are told in verse nineteen, was also *not understood*. Faith has not yet grown in their heart, because they were hardened (blinded) to the truth. Leading them through a prayer would be merely a confession without faith.

The second soil described is also unprepared to bring forth the fruit of saving faith.

> "But he that received the seed into stony places, the same is he that heareth the word, and anon with joy receiveth it; Yet hath he not root in himself, **but dureth for a while**: for when tribulation or persecution ariseth because of the word, **by and by he is offended**." (Matthew 13:20-21)

There is indeed a superficial belief, or head knowledge, that springs up and *resembles* saving faith, but the seed of the word is not able to take root and so is not able to produce the fruit of saving faith, but instead withers and dies.

Even though these may appear at first to receive the seed, there is no depth to their belief, so what springs up remains above ground, not penetrating the soil of the heart. Having *no roots* to sustain it, when the sun comes up it is scorched and withered away.

Anyone who has ever had a garden knows that seeds often sprout up but then fail, especially if they do not have sufficient roots to nourish and hydrate them. If these have *no roots* and are *unable to sustain* the plant, they are not going to produce fruit, in this case, the fruit of saving faith.

> "And some fell upon a rock; and as soon as it was sprung up, it withered away, **because it lacked moisture**." (Luke 8:6)

What may have *looked* very much like saving faith, was only superficial belief that sprung up quickly, *then died*. It withered away because, as we are told, it had no roots and therefore "lacked moisture" (Luke 8:6).

> "He that believeth on me, as the Scripture hath said, out of his belly shall flow rivers of living water." (John 7:38)

We might compare them to those who very excitedly come to church for a time, even involving themselves in ministries, but eventually lose interest and fall away. They may have religious zeal, but they lack the moisture of the water of life (the Holy Spirit), and so wither away without producing the fruit of saving faith.

Saving faith brings *eternal* life, *not temporary* life. We know that this could *not* be saving faith, because it sprouted up quickly but then withered away. Not only did it *not* produce fruit; *it died*. Unless we are willing to believe that salvation can be lost, how could we possibly suggest that this was salvation at all.

Because of this superficial interest, however, many wrongly interpret this seed as one who *got saved* but is now living carnally and simply no longer producing works of righteousness.

As we have already seen, these did not simply stop producing fruits, what sprouted up within them died before it ever produced any genuine fruit *at all*.

When the seed of the word is sown into the heart of the unsaved, the *only* fruit that can grow there is faith. If the seed of the word sown into the heart of the unsaved dies before it can produce *fruit,* then they do not yet have saving faith.

Suggesting that these are carnal Christians affords

another problem. When Paul addressed carnality (envy, strife, division...etc.) in the Corinthian Church, he was addressing those continuing *in the church*, who were behaving carnally, not those who left the church never to be seen again. These that sprung up in the stony soil are not carnal believers, but those who left the faith. We are told that these *only dureth for a while* because they were offended and fell away.

"They on the rock are they, which, when they hear, receive the word with joy; and these have no root, which for a while believe, **and in time of temptation fall away**." (Luke 8:13)

"But he that received the seed into stony places, the same is he that heareth the word, and anon with joy receiveth it; Yet hath he not root in himself, **but dureth for a while**: for when tribulation or persecution ariseth because of the word, **by and by he is offended**." (Matthew 13:20-21)

According to Strong's Exhaustive Concordance of the Bible, both terms, *offended* and *fall away*, used interchangeably in these parallel passages convey the idea of apostacy. This is not merely a loss of interest, and lack of good works; this is a departure from the professed faith.

Offended σκανδαλίζω skandalízō, skan-dal-id'-zo; from G4625; to entrap, i.e. trip up (figuratively, stumble (transitively) or entice to sin, **apostasy** or displeasure):— (make to) offend. b. "to cause a person to begin to distrust and desert one whom he ought to trust and obey; to cause to fall away," (Strong's Greek Lexicon (KJV)." Blue Letter Bible. Web. 28 Sep, 2019.)

Fall away ἀφίστημι aphístēmi, af-is'-tay-mee; from G575 and G2476; to remove, i.e. (actively) instigate to revolt; usually (reflexively) to desist, desert, etc.:—depart, draw (fall) away, refrain, withdraw self, c. to **fall away, become faithless**. (Strong's Greek Lexicon (KJV)." Blue Letter Bible. Web. 28 Sep, 2019.)

These were not carnal Christians, because they did not continue in the faith as Christians at all. These, as we are told, *fell away* from the faith. When they faced tribulation and persecution because of the word, they were ashamed and driven to renounce the faith, abandoning it.

A failure to continue in the faith, according to Scripture, is a clear indication that salvation was not genuine.

> "They went out from us, but they were not of us; for if they had been of us, they would no doubt have continued with us: but they went out, **that they might be made manifest that they were not all of us.**" (1 John 2:19)

We are told that the seed sown among thorns, also bringeth *no fruit* to perfection. It does not produce saving faith.

> "He also that received seed among the thorns is he that heareth the word; and the **care of this world, and the deceitfulness of riches, choke the word, and he becometh unfruitful.**" (Matthew 13:20-22)

> "And that which fell among thorns are they, which, when they have heard, go forth, and are choked with cares and riches and pleasures of this life, and bring **no fruit to perfection.**" (Luke 8:14)

These too, bring forth *no* fruit, which means *no* saving faith- no salvation. Although these also seem at first to be willing to hear the word, receiving it with joy; appearances can be deceiving. A heart that is filled with sin and the cares of this world also will not allow the seed of the word to grow into saving faith.

The soil is still rocky and hard, where only thorns and briars grow and will not allow the word to take root. The pleasures of the world and desire for sin choke out what word has been heard, not allowing it to bring forth the fruit of saving faith. The only thing this soil allows to grow is thorns and briars. We read in Hebrews, the end of such things:

> "But that which beareth thorns and briers **is rejected, and is nigh unto cursing; whose end is to be burned.**" (Hebrews 6:8)

> "Even so **every** good tree bringeth forth good fruit; but a corrupt tree bringeth forth evil fruit. A good tree cannot bring forth evil fruit, neither can a corrupt tree bring forth good fruit. **Every tree that bringeth not forth good fruit is hewn down, and cast into the fire**. (Matthew 7:17-19)

None of the soils we have looked at so far have produced any fruit at all. Matthew tells us that every good tree brings forth good fruit. The tree that brings forth no good fruit is cast into the fire. If there is no fruit, can it be a good tree? Certainly not. If there is no fruit, then these are not saved and destined for eternal life, but to be burned in hell.

I know that it is difficult for many who have seen this played out to accept the truth of these Scriptures, but for the love of souls, I pray that you will please put aside your own experiences and emotional investments and simply believe the word of God.

It's easy to see how we might initially mistake someone who seems to receive the word gladly, as having genuine faith. That is why it is so important that we *do not* give false assurances to everyone that professes faith. Only the Lord can discern the soil of their hearts. We can only watch and observe the fruits or lack thereof produced by these professors.

"But that on the good ground are they, which in an honest and good heart, having heard the word, keep it, and bring forth fruit with patience." (Luke 8:15)

The good soil of the heart that has been broken up in repentance toward God allows the seed of the word of God to take root and grow, producing faith in good measure.

"But he that received seed into the good ground is he that heareth the word, and understandeth it; which also beareth fruit, and bringeth forth, some an hundredfold, some sixty, some thirty." (Matthew 13:23)

So, we see that the way a man receives the seed of the word depends upon the condition of his heart toward God.

"The LORD is nigh unto them that are of a broken heart; and saveth such as be of a contrite spirit." (Psalms 34:18)

Only the good soil produces the fruit of saving faith. Notice also that this is the only soil that we are told *understands the word* or has come to a knowledge of the truth. When the word of God is sown in the heart of a repentant sinner, readily willing to hear and receive that word of life, the Holy Spirit, through the preaching of the word, enlightens the understanding, bringing him to a knowledge of the truth. The moment that saving faith is produced, the Holy Spirit brings him to new life and seals him.

"In whom ye also **trusted, after that ye heard** the word of truth, the gospel of your salvation: in whom also **after that ye believed, ye were sealed** with that holy

Spirit of promise" (Ephesians 1:13)

It is then that "out of the abundance of the heart the mouth speaketh" (Matthew 12:34), confessing the faith that has saved us.

• The repentant sinner (the good soil) becomes willing to hear the words of life in order to be reconciled with God. "If any man have ears to hear, let him hear." (Mark 7:16)
• The seed of the word is sown through preaching. "… it pleased God by the foolishness of preaching to save them that believe." (1 Corinthians 1:21)
• The Holy Spirit enlightens the understanding. "Who will have all men to be saved, **and to come unto the knowledge of the truth**." (1 Timothy 2:4)
• Faith (belief) brings salvation. The incorruptible seed of the word produces the fruit of salvation. "In whom ye also trusted, after that ye heard **the word of truth**, the gospel of your salvation: in whom also after that ye believed, ye were sealed with that holy Spirit of promise," (Ephesians 1:13) Notice that word of truth cannot be separated from the gospel.
• Confession is made of that salvation. "For with the heart man believeth unto righteousness; and with the mouth confession is made unto salvation." (Romans 10:10)

Unbelief to Belief

As I mentioned previously, there is a movement within modern Christianity that attempts to redefine repentance as merely a change from unbelief in Christ to belief, essentially eliminating the need for repentance toward God, from sin. After examining the parable of the sower it's easy to see the fatal error of teaching that repentance is merely turning from unbelief to belief. A refusal to turn from sin, to God in repentance is evidence of hardness of heart or spiritual blindness.

Those who will not repent toward God simply *cannot* believe in Christ as their Savior.

Redefining repentance as turning from unbelief to belief may make it easier to collect decisions for Christ; but before the gospel can truly produce saving faith there must be a willingness to hear God.

This deceptive teaching, however, has found its way into even the most Bible-believing churches. I recently heard one preacher say that teaching that repentance includes turning from sin, or even sorrow for sin, is false teaching. He redefined repentance as a change of mind that merely *anticipates* a change of action (turning from sin).

He explained that turning from sin only happened after salvation. The idea that man cannot repent of sin until he is regenerated finds its roots in Calvinism's doctrine of total depravity/inability, but also lends itself nicely to Easy Believism in this aspect.

He would be correct in stating that repentance is not either one of these things alone; but genuine, biblical repentance involves both sorrow for sin and turning from sin. Repentance is *not* an eradication of sin or even freedom from the power of sin. That can only come through salvation in Christ by the power of the Holy Spirit. Repentance, however, is a godly sorrow over sin, and turning from its destructive path, toward God instead.

Repentance is a change of mind that does not merely *anticipate* but *initiates* a change of action. Repentance is making straight the path, clearing away all the bramble and brush, the cares of the world and deceitfulness of sin, and preparing the way for the Lord. Repentance does not end there though. After salvation, the believer is empowered to not only turn from sin but be freed from sin. The born-again believer in Christ is dead to sin.

Repentance that does not produce a change of action is not repentance. God himself is our example that repentance initiates a change of action.

> "Now therefore let me alone, that my wrath may wax hot against them, and that I may consume them: and I will make of thee a great nation." (Exodus 32:10)

> "And the LORD repented of the evil which he thought to do unto his people." (Exodus 32:14)

Because of Israel's stiff-necked disobedience, God wanted to wipe them out and begin again with only Moses, making of him a great nation. Moses pleaded with God and God repented. He did not merely change his mind; he also changed his course of action. His repentance meant that he did not do that which he had thought to do, which was to destroy the people of Israel. Another example would be the punishment of David's numbering of Israel.

> "And God sent an angel unto Jerusalem to destroy it: and as he was destroying, the LORD beheld, and he repented him of the evil, and said to the angel that destroyed, It is enough, stay now thine hand." (1Chronicles 21:15)

God stopped the angel. He changed his mind and did not do what he had begun to do. His repentance initiated a change of action.

When God repented that he had made Saul king, he immediately commanded Samuel to go and anoint a new king who would replace him.

> "If it do evil in my sight, that it obey not my voice, then I will repent of the good, wherewith I said I would benefit them." (Jeremiah 18:10)

When God told Israel that if they did evil, he would repent of his goodness and blessings to them, did he merely change his mind? Did he continue to bless them with good things when he repented? No. Whenever God repented, he also changed his action. When he repented of the good that he intended for them, it meant that he would no longer do it.

Repentance is not hard to understand. What makes it so difficult and confusing is all the false teachings people invent to try to get around it. Repentance is not simply agreeing with God that our sin is sin but turning from it *to him*.

The cares of this world and the deceitfulness of sin can easily harden us against the truth, blinding us. Although I'm praying it will not be so; I know that it is very possible that some even reading this today will be so indoctrinated with the teachings of modern Christianity that they are no longer able to see the true gospel of Jesus Christ.

> "Take heed therefore how ye hear: for whosoever hath, to him shall be given; and whosoever hath not, from him shall be taken even that which he seemeth to have." (Luke 8:18)

We will give account to God for how we handle his word and present his truth.

CHAPTER 4
DO OUR CONVERTS GLORIFY GOD?

In soul winning, I continually meet people who claim to be saved already. Very rarely do I meet any who evidence biblical salvation by a changed life, a steadfast continuation in doctrine and fellowship with believers, a holy lifestyle or even Bible reading.

The majority live in sin and open rebellion against God, or continued idolatry and confusion about the way of salvation. Most often, these claiming salvation were never even willing to be baptized as a testimony to their profession of faith; but were still assured by someone that because they had prayed a prayer at one time in their life, they were indeed saved.

I once spoke with a young Catholic woman who was extremely confused about the way of salvation. Although she was still trusting in her works and idolatry to save her, she told me that a Christian woman had led her through a prayer and told her that she was saved. She said that she repeated all the special words that the lady had said. She could not remember what they were, but that the Christian woman had told her that she was now indeed saved. This poor young woman simply added this magical prayer to her own efforts toward earning salvation. How utterly shameful that we who know the way of salvation through faith in Christ alone, would be so careless with it.

I could tell you many more of the same stories. Sadly, this has become the norm. Many times, I have personally heard soul winners lead people with little or no interest in God, through a sinner's prayer and pronounce them saved.

Some of the more fortunate ones who grow up in the church eventually come to saving faith; but by their own admission, struggle with the reality of salvation many times over. Most only come to an assurance in their adult years, after much fearful searching and after coming to genuine repentance and faith. It is then that God becomes real to them and they begin to show genuine evidences of salvation. Often, they will refer to this as a recommitment.

It breaks my heart that we have made the precious gospel of Christ nothing more than a quick gimmick used to coerce people (often the unbelieving) into simply repeating a superstitious prayer that we suggest they now trust for their salvation. How sad that so many today, have been deceived by this false gospel.

Although I regularly hear Christians praising God and giving him the glory for souls like these that they have *led to the Lord*; I often wonder how what we are doing can possibly glorify God.

For this reason, I'd like to ask a very pointed question that only you can answer for yourself: Do your converts (those you lead to Christ through prayer) bring glory to God? This may seem like a ridiculous question. You may even be thinking, "It always glorifies God when people pray to accept Jesus." Does it?

Let me apologize ahead of time for what I'm about to ask next. This is as difficult to ask as it is to hear, but I believe it is necessary if we are going to address the problem. If your converts are not glorifying God, then who are they glorifying? You? Satan?

The questions below should help you to answer these questions.

-**Do your converts publicly testify to the church of their conversion by believer's baptism?** Or is yours the only testimony the church ever hears?

> "Then they that gladly received his word were baptized…" (Acts 2:41a)

-**Do your converts join themselves to the church?** Or are they never seen again?

> "…and the same day there were added unto them about three thousand souls." (Acts 2:41b)

-**Do your converts serve God?** Or do they serve Satan?

> "Know ye not, that to whom ye yield yourselves servants to obey, his servants ye are to whom ye obey; whether of sin unto death, or of obedience unto righteousness?" (Romans 6:16)

-**Do your converts glorify the name of Christ to the world through their lives?** Or do their lives cause non-believers to blaspheme his name?

> "Thou that makest thy boast of the law, through breaking the law dishonourest thou God? For the name of God is blasphemed among the Gentiles through you, as it is written." (Romans 2:23-24)

-**Do your converts strive to live holy lives as a chaste bride prepared for Christ?** Or do they live like the Devil?

> "For I am jealous over you with godly jealousy: for I have espoused you to one husband, that I may present you as a chaste virgin to Christ." (2 Corinthians 11:2)

-**Do your converts show new life as new creatures?** Or do they go on just the same as they always have?

> "Therefore if any man be in Christ, he is a new creature: old things are passed away; behold, all things are become new." (2 Corinthians 5:17)

-**Do your converts show the fruit of the Spirit?** Or do they only show works of the flesh?

> "Now the works of the flesh are manifest, which are these; Adultery, fornication, uncleanness, lasciviousness, Idolatry, witchcraft, hatred, variance, emulations, wrath, strife, seditions, heresies, Envyings, murders, drunkenness, revellings, and such like: of the which I tell you before, as **I have also told you in time past, that they which do such things shall not inherit the kingdom of God**." (Galatians 5:19-21)

-**Do your converts show any evidence at all that their names are indeed written in the lamb's book of life?** Or are they only written in the back of your Bible?

> "And whosoever was not found written in the book of life was cast into the lake of fire." (Revelation 20:15)

If you are honest with yourself, then like most soul winners today, your answers were probably discouraging.

Can we honestly believe that God is glorified through these converts?

Now comes the tough question: Are you content to continue claiming converts such as these for the Lord, and to present them to Christ as his bride?

The apostle Paul was concerned with how his converts were living as Christians. He wrote to the churches, admonishing them to be holy as a chaste bride for Christ. Are we doing likewise? I think we must admit that we are not, because many of our converts never join themselves to the church. As a matter of fact, we often have no expectations of our converts, because most are never even seen again.

Our converts are most often, in word only. If we are

going to be honest, the only ones they glorify are the soul winners claiming them; yet we act as though we have done our duty in making converts such as these.

We offer to God, not our best efforts, not the cream of the crop which we have diligently sown, watered and brought to harvest, but our withered crops that will not bear fruit, servants who will not serve.

We tell our converts that they can become the sons of God if they will accept Jesus through prayer. They willingly take us up on that offer, claiming heaven as their prize, but they will not honor God as their father.

> "A son honoureth his father, and a servant his master: if then I be a father, where is mine honour? and if I be a master, where is my fear? saith the LORD of hosts unto you, O priests, that despise my name. And ye say, Wherein have we despised thy name? Ye offer polluted bread upon mine altar; and ye say, Wherein have we polluted thee? In that ye say, The table of the LORD is contemptible. And if ye offer the blind for sacrifice, is it not evil? and if ye offer the lame and sick, is it not evil? offer it now unto thy governor; will he be pleased with thee, or accept thy person? saith the LORD of hosts. (Malachi 1:6-8)

How can we expect God to be pleased? Have we not wearied him instead?

> "Ye have wearied the LORD with your words. Yet ye say, Wherein have we wearied him? When ye say, Every one that doeth evil is good in the sight of the LORD, and he delighteth in them;" (Malachi 2:17)

Not only do we claim that every one of these who will not honor God or serve him is yet good in his sight; but we strengthen the hands of the wicked to do even more wickedly with an assurance that they are now saved.

> "Because with lies ye have made the heart of the righteous sad, whom I have not made sad; and strengthened the hands of the wicked, **that he should not return from his wicked way, by promising him life:**" (Ezekiel 13:22)

It's time for a change! The Sinner's Prayer is no guarantee of salvation. It represents a faulty view of salvation, a view that salvation is received by prayer, rather than by faith. We are not saved by a magical prayer! If there is no repentance or faith, or if there is no understanding of the gospel message, then the prayer is worthless.

Sowing and Reaping

This generation of soul winners, like no other, now expects to present an edited, shallow, gospel message and reap a harvest instantly. We go out knocking on doors with the intention of winning souls in under three minutes, which might be possible if someone else had already sown and watered the seed of the word. But most often, we meet people who have no interest in God or the gospel but have already been pronounced saved by another overly zealous soul winner.

These who are overcome in sin, whose hearts are hardened or indifferent to God need someone with the courage to plow up the stony ground of their hearts with the preaching of the word and allow the Holy Spirit to convict them. They quite simply need to see that they are lost.

It used to be a common expression in Christianity that you must get them lost before you get them saved. Somehow, we've forgotten that truth. If we are going to push for any decision, shouldn't it be for repentance toward God, admonishing them in the fear of the Lord?

We cannot all reap. Someone must sow, and someone must water as well. Paul understood this principle. He was content to sow and allow another to water and for God to get the glory. Paul clearly was not interested in quick numbers.

> "I have planted, Apollos watered; but God gave the increase." (1 Corinthians 3:6)

If God calls us to sow the seed, or water where someone else has sown without any applause, are we willing to do so? Will we allow the Holy Spirit to work in their hearts? Or are we only interested in securing professions at any cost? Are our quick decisions and prayers really for the love of their souls? How many of these poor souls are actually better off for having heard our false gospel of *just say this prayer*?

> "For if after they have escaped the pollutions of the world through the knowledge of the Lord and Saviour Jesus Christ, they are again entangled therein, and overcome, **the latter end is worse with them than the beginning.**" (2 Peter 2:20).

I have heard some suggest that we just get them saved and God will deal with their sin later; but a false profession may remove any budding conviction they have. Removing their fear of the Lord by giving assurance of salvation can even lead them farther from God then before. We must allow the Holy Spirit to work in their lives.

There was a lady once who had visited our church a couple of times. One day she came forward at the invitation, bawling her eyes out. She was the very picture of brokenness and repentance. (Obviously, not all who are under conviction will be so visibly stirred. Most are not as emotional.) When I took her into one of the back rooms to counsel her, I asked why she had come forward. She told me that she wanted to get saved, and very openly discussed the conviction she was under.

She revealed that she was living in sin with her boyfriend

and was greatly convicted. She wanted to know what she should do. I told her that if God was convicting her, and she knew that she was in sin, she should be obedient to God and turn from that sin somehow. Sadly, that was not at all something she was willing to do.

It seemed she wanted relief from the condemnation of her sin but did not desire to turn from it. Conviction is *not* the same thing as repentance. Many people come to church and are convicted about their sin through the preaching of the word. The difference between those who come to salvation and those who do not is what they choose to do with that conviction. This is where the free will of man enters in. Will they choose to agree with God about their sin and turn from it? Or will they attempt to escape the discomfort of conviction by turning from God instead?

She certainly seemed to have Holy Spirit conviction, but conviction alone is not enough. There must also be a repentant heart. She chose to turn from God rather than from her sin.

> "Salvation is far from the wicked: for they seek not thy statutes" (Psalms 119:155).

I believe that this dear lady sincerely desired relief from her conviction, but it would have been a great disservice to her for me to do that. I cannot forgive her sin or excuse it. None of us can. We do not have the power or the authority. All I could do was agree with God that her sin was indeed sin and needed to be turned from.

I could not lead her to believe that she could continue in her sin, and simply pray a prayer to make it all ok. To pronounce her saved merely because she expressed conviction of sin, would have been foolish. I counseled her to be obedient to God and to continue seeking to hear his word, but I did not attempt to soothe her conviction, or lead her to believe that she was saved.

I reminded her of the clear gospel presentation she had

heard during the service and made sure she understood that salvation is by grace through faith and not of works. I urged her to turn from her sin, to God and be reconciled to him through faith in Christ and let her know that I was available to talk anytime, if she needed further counsel.

She left that day with the knowledge of God's rightful condemnation of her sin, and aware of the remedy for it.

I know many would disagree with me for *blowing* such a great opportunity to *get someone saved*. They would suggest that I should have simply gotten her saved and then worried about her sin and repentance later.

She left there, not with a soothed conscience, but with a heavy load of conviction still upon her shoulders. Most importantly though, she left with the knowledge of how to be saved when she was ready to be reconciled to God. Although her sorrow did appear to be sincere, and it saddened me to see her leave feeling no better, I had no way of knowing whether it was godly sorrow or worldly sorrow.

There are many reasons that people come forward and claim to want salvation, many even with tears such as this dear lady. The only way we can even have any indication, is to see what comes from it.

> "For godly sorrow worketh **repentance to salvation** not to be repented of: but the sorrow of the world **worketh death**" (2 Corinthians 7:10).

For several years, her circumstances did not change. She continued to live in sin and continued to be unsaved. This leads me to believe that her sorrow at that time was not godly sorrow, but worldly sorrow.

Her sorrow did not lead to repentance and salvation, but to a continuance in sin and destruction. What we do with conviction is what shows whether it is truly godly sorrow that worketh repentance or not.

Godly sorrow that worketh repentance causes us to change our mind about our sin. Because of God's word, we see our sin as God sees it, exceedingly sinful, and see God's just condemnation as right and true. No longer can we excuse our sin or defend it or fight for our right to continue in it, and so we desire to turn from our sin in submission to God's authority.

Worldly sorrow may feel that same conviction of sin; but is not willing to submit to God. Instead of agreeing with him and turning from sin, those under conviction choose to turn from God and *cling* to their sin. Often, they defend it and argue against God's condemnation of it.

Rather than repent, they attempt to ease their conscience by hiding from God, refusing to hear his word. They may stop going to church or spending time with those who would bring conviction, and even surround themselves with others who participate in the same sin to buffer the conviction. But we know that we can never really hide from God. He sees us wherever we are and can convict us even by our own conscience.

While we should warn people of the urgency of turning to God, we must give people time to come to the place of repentance; because without repentance toward God there is no salvation. I could have easily created a false convert that day by leading her through a prayer and assuring her of salvation, but chose to let her walk away instead, as I believe Christ himself would have done. We see an example of this in the story of the rich young ruler.

> "And when he was gone forth into the way, there came one running, and kneeled to him, and asked him, Good Master, what shall I do that I may inherit eternal life? And Jesus said unto him, Why callest thou me good? there is none good but one, that is, God. Thou knowest the commandments, Do not commit adultery, Do not kill, Do not steal, Do not bear false witness, Defraud not, Honour thy father and mother. And he answered and said unto him, Master, all these have I observed from my youth. Then Jesus beholding him

loved him, and said unto him, One thing thou lackest: go thy way, sell whatsoever thou hast, and give to the poor, and thou shalt have treasure in heaven: and come, take up the cross, and follow me. And he was sad at that saying, and went away grieved: for he had great possessions" (Mark 10:17-22).

This ruler came, not with tears, but with self-righteousness. He was confident that he was already prepared to receive eternal life. Jesus, however demanded from him, repentance of his sin. Jesus called him to sell all his possessions and give them to the poor. His choice reveals how far short he had come from keeping all the commandments he claimed to have kept.

He went away sorrowful because he chose to love his riches more than God, and himself more than others. This man was no more interested in turning from his sin than the lady I spoke with, and so went away, not with an assurance of salvation, but grieved with the knowledge of his own conviction. Whatever reasons others might come up with, I'll choose to follow Jesus and his example instead. He knows far better how to deal with men's hearts than we do.

How did Jesus deal with those who were unrepentant or self-righteous? Jesus did not offer an easy way out to the rich young ruler, and we must resist the urge to do so ourselves. Did he ever just ignore sin and welcome them into salvation? No. He always addressed sin and the need for repentance. We need to do the same. We must be patient enough to help prepare the soil of their hearts

Sometimes we are so eager to give others the good news that we are unwilling to let them walk away as Jesus did. As soon as they show the slightest awareness of sin, we rush to offer our prayer and assure them of salvation. I am not suggesting in any way that we discourage people from making decisions to turn to God, or that we suggest that they wait, or that repentance is a lengthy process. For some it's instantaneous. But, for those who are not repentant, leading them through a meaningless prayer can cause permanent harm.

Why would they ever repent if they believe they are forgiven already? Why would they continue seeking a cure for their disease if we convinced them they are already cured? It is like telling them that they are healthy and have nothing to worry about when they are in fact dying. It is promising them life when God has not promised them life.

That does not mean we withhold the good news of salvation in Christ. Just as with the lady who came forward in tears, it is important to make them aware of the gospel, but *that gospel must include repentance.*

I don't know about you, but I'd rather have one genuine convert than a thousand who have only prayed a prayer and will not live for Christ.

CHAPTER 5
BE YE HOLY

"The disciple is not above his master: but every one that is perfect shall be as his master." (Luke 6:40)

We will never make disciples better than we are Christians. Our converts will only rise to the level of the standard we set.

"Whether therefore ye eat, or drink, or whatsoever ye do, do all to the glory of God." (1 Corinthians 10:31)

Man was created by God to glorify God. How better to glorify him than by striving to be like him? God's primary attribute is holiness. That is why we are told to be holy as well.

"Because it is written, **Be ye holy; for I am holy**." (1 Peter 1:16).

Is being holy something that is beyond our reach? In today's world of Easy Believism where everyone who prays a prayer is counted as a believer, and then returns to a life of sin; it seems that way. Holiness is rarely preached or emphasized today. Many professing Christians even within the church wrestle with drunkenness, immorality, and other habitual sins for years. They struggle and fail and cannot seem to get victory over their sin.

Often we commiserate with them and excuse their struggle, quoting Paul: "For that which I do I allow not: for what I would, that do I not; but what I hate, that do I." "O wretched man that I am!" (Romans 7:15 & 24)

We comfort them (and ourselves) with the thought that since Paul struggled with sin this way, we will all struggle and none of us will be able to attain to the holiness we seek. I have heard it preached that we can aim for holiness and righteousness toward God, but sadly, we will only continue to fall short because of the sin still dwelling in our flesh. But, is this what Paul was telling us? Was Paul crying out as a born-again Christian struggling against *captivity to sin?*

Clearly, Paul was a believer when he wrote this, so it is assumed by most that what he is speaking of is his present struggle as a believer. This seems to be the standard teaching of the church, often used to prove that Christians can still sin after salvation.

While it is true that we as Christians will still have sin dwelling within our flesh for as long as we are in these mortal bodies, I do not believe that this is the intended message of this passage. If it were, it would be in direct contradiction to everything he wrote in the previous chapter.

Everything that Paul discusses in chapter seven and even into chapter eight is a continuation of what he was speaking of in chapter six. In order to rightly understand what Paul is saying in chapter seven, we must look back at chapter six.

Paul opens chapter six with the question? "Shall we continue in sin that grace may abound?" (Romans 6:1) What is his answer? "God forbid. How shall we, that are dead to sin, live any longer therein?" (Romans 6:2)

He is telling these believers at Rome that we are dead to sin, and he that is dead to sin is freed from sin. How then shall we continue in sin? God forbid that we should do so.

> "Knowing this, that our old man is crucified with him, that the body of sin might be destroyed, **that henceforth we should not serve sin. For he that is dead is freed from sin**." (Romans 6:6-7)

Paul explains that as believers we are dead to sin, therefore, we should not allow sin to reign over us. We are no longer sold under sin that we should yield ourselves to obey it; we have been purchased by Christ and set free from sin. Sin *no longer has dominion* (rule or power) over us.

"Let not sin therefore reign in your mortal body, that ye should obey it in the lusts thereof. Neither yield ye your members as instruments of unrighteousness unto sin: but yield yourselves unto God, as those that are alive from the dead, and your members as instruments of righteousness unto God." (Romans 6:12-13)

We now have a choice, we can yield ourselves as servants of sin, or we can yield ourselves as instruments of righteousness to God, because we are now servants of God.

"But now being made free from sin, and become servants to God, ye have your fruit unto holiness, and the end everlasting life." (Romans 6:22)

Paul tells us that as born-again believers, we are freed from sin, being dead to it because of salvation in Christ. We now can indeed bring forth fruits of righteousness to God *because sin no longer has power over us!* This does not at all mean that sin has been eradicated from our flesh, but that the *power* of sin has been crucified with Christ. *We are no longer slaves to sin!*

"For sin **shall not have dominion** over you: for ye are not under the law, but under grace." (Romans 6:14)

Believers in Christ are no longer under the power of the flesh, but of the Spirit, just as they are no longer under the law, but under grace. He goes on to explain that while we were yet in the flesh, the motions of sin were clearly brought to light and condemned by the law, working in our bodies to bring forth death. Now however, as born-again believers with the indwelling Spirit, we are no longer in the flesh, and are freed from *its power* as well as *its condemnation* by the law.

"For when we were in the flesh, the motions of sins, which were by the law, did work in our members to bring forth fruit unto death. **But now** we are delivered from the law, that **being dead wherein we were held; that we should serve in newness of spirit,** and not in the oldness of the letter." (Romans 7:5-6)

We as believers are no longer dead *by* the law but are dead *to* the law's condemnation; and we are no longer in the flesh, but in the Spirit if we are saved. Paul goes into chapter seven discussing the purpose of the law and reflecting on the work that the law did in his heart *prior* to salvation. Few would argue against the fact that Paul is referring to the past in this Scripture.

"For I was alive without the law once: but when the commandment came, sin revived, and I died. And the commandment, which was ordained to life, I found to be unto death. For sin, taking occasion by the commandment, deceived me, and by it slew me. Wherefore the law is holy, and the commandment holy, and just, and good. Was then that which is good made death unto me? God forbid. But sin, that it might appear sin, working death in me by that which is good; that sin by the commandment might become exceeding sinful." (Romans 7:9-13)

Paul describes how the law showed him his sin. As he strived to become righteous through the works of the law, it instead exposed the sin within him. That which he thought to be life and righteousness instead proved his sin and unrighteousness.

Because of his sinful flesh, even when he desired to do good, sin was present. His works were all corrupted (like filthy rags) by his sin. The more this lost man attempted to attain to the righteousness of God by the law, the more condemnation of sin it brought. This is the purpose of the law for every sinner, to see their sin as God does and to come to a knowledge of their need for a Savior.

In verse fourteen, however, Paul's language switches from past to present tense, which naturally confuses many.

"For we know that **the law is spiritual: but I am carnal**, sold under sin." (Romans 7:14)

He does not say, I *was* carnal, but says, I *am* carnal. This is not to show that he is speaking of his present condition however, as a born-again Christian, but only to give his memory a voice.

How do we know this? Because he also says that *in his carnal state* he is sold under sin. That phrase literally means sold (as merchandise or into slavery) under (by) sin. What he is saying is *that as a carnal* man he was owned by sin as a slave to sin. This could never be said of a born-again believer because we have just been told in chapter six that sin no longer has dominion over us. We have been freed from the power of sin so that we may now serve God. We have been purchased by the blood of Christ; and sin is no longer our master.

Paul goes on to say:

"For I know that in me (that is, in my flesh,) dwelleth no good thing: for to will is present with me; but how to perform that which is good I find not. For the good that I would I do not: but the evil which I would not, that I do. Now if I do that I would not, it is no more I that do it, but sin that dwelleth in me. I find then a law, that, when I would do good, evil is present with me. For I delight in the law of God after the inward man: But I see another law in my members, warring against the law of my mind, and **bringing me into captivity to the law of sin** which is in my members." (Romans 7:18-23)

Notice that Paul speaks here of the law of sin bringing him into captivity against the desires of his mind. Paul has already established our freedom from the power of sin. Is he now saying that sin has the power to bring him into captivity as a born-again Christian? Certainly not! Sin no longer has dominion over us.

Paul was not crying, "oh woe is me…" or "o wretched man that I am", as a saved man held captive by sin. This was the cry of his heart prior to being made free from the law and from sin. The harder he tried to do good, the greater his sin appeared. The more he sought to serve God through the works of the law, the greater his condemnation. That which he thought was life became *death* to him.

Surely, we cannot think that this is true for the born-again believer in Christ. Believers are no longer under the condemnation of spiritual death, because **"there is therefore now no condemnation** for them that are in Christ that walk not after the flesh but after the Spirit." (Romans 8:1)

We cannot be in the flesh and in the Spirit at the same time because they are contrary to each other.

> "For the flesh lusteth against the Spirit, and the Spirit against the flesh: and these are contrary the one to the other:" (Galatians 5:17)

If we are in the flesh, we work the works of the flesh, being under the law and its condemnation. The flesh and the law are both opposed to spiritual things and not compatible with grace.

> "But if ye be led of the Spirit, ye are not under the

law." (Galatians 5:18)

If we are in the Spirit and under grace, we are no longer under the law because we are no longer in the flesh. The Spirit within us now stands against the desires and the works of the flesh.

> "And **they that are Christ's have crucified the flesh** with the affections and lusts." (Galatians 5:24)

Paul was not bemoaning his inability to serve God but contrasting the bondage of sin and death for the unbeliever with the freedom of new life in Christ. He was praising God for the freedom from sin that has been provided through the indwelling Holy Spirit. He was attempting to empower these Christians in Rome with the knowledge that if they are indwelt with the Holy Spirit of Christ, they are now *freed from sin's captivity*!

It would not be consistent with the context of the passage for Paul to be in one chapter, speaking of freedom from sin's power and in the next bemoaning his captivity to the law of sin. He has gone into detail explaining that we are dead to sin and that the law of sin no longer has dominion over us. Again, we are no longer in the flesh, but in the Spirit and no longer under the law, but under grace.

If we were to believe that Paul was speaking of his present struggle against sin, as a born-again believer, this entire passage would be a glaring contradiction to the truths he previously established. He then goes on to say:

> "O wretched man that I am! who shall deliver me from the body of this death? *I thank God **through** Jesus Christ our Lord.* So then with the mind I myself serve the law of God; but with the flesh the law of sin." (Romans 7:24-25)

Paul states clearly that at the time in which he is

referring, he was serving the law of God and the law of sin. As believers *we neither* serve the law of God *or* the law of sin.

> "For the law of the Spirit of life in Christ Jesus hath made me **free** from **the law of sin and death**." (Romans 8:2)

What is it that frees us from the law, and from sin? Salvation in Christ, which brought the indwelling Spirit that freed us from the law of sin and death. Paul could only be referring to the time before his salvation, when he says that he was serving the law and that sin brought death.

Chapter seven illustrates how that the law had its purpose for a time but could not produce the fruits of righteousness. What the law could not do, in that it was not able to overcome the flesh, the indwelling Spirit can do. New life in Christ which frees us from the law of God and the law of sin, also brings life and service to God. Which is why he goes on to say:

> "For what the law could not do, in that it was weak through the flesh, God sending his own Son in the likeness of sinful flesh, and for sin, **condemned sin in the flesh**: (Romans 8:3)

As much as this may conflict with what many of us within Christianity have been taught, this passage is not describing the struggles of Paul as a carnal Christian striving to enter chapter eight victory! Chapter eight makes it clear that *all* genuine Christians are chapter eight Christians, *or they are not Christians at all!*

> "But ye are not in the flesh, but in the Spirit, **if** so be that the Spirit of God dwell in you. Now **if any man have not the Spirit of Christ, he is none of his**." (Romans 8:9)

If we are born again by the Holy Spirit, we *are* in the Spirit and *no longer in the flesh*. Anyone who does not have the Spirit of Christ, is simply not a Christian.

Paul wrote this, not to excuse sin and to show how far short we come from pleasing God, but to empower believers to see that we *can* live holy lives despite the sin that still dwells within our flesh. *We are dead to sin, and alive unto God* by the Holy Spirit and able to bring forth fruits of righteousness.

Is it any wonder we have churches full of weak and powerless professing Christians, overcome in sin, when we do not even understand the incredible message of hope and power and righteousness Paul is giving? We use his words instead, to lower the bar for all, excusing sin and complacency. "O Woe is me! O wretched man that I am."

This passage should be showing Christians that we *can* overcome sin. It is not a matter of how high we set our sights, or how much we rely on the Holy Spirit that determines whether we are freed from the captivity of sin. It is whether we are saved.

The Holy Spirit was able to do that which the law could not, which was to overcome sin, and death.

Just like Peter's transformation after the Holy Spirit came. Before his regeneration, Peter believed in who Jesus was, and claimed that he would even die for him; but when persecution and danger came, he denied Christ and fled in shame. In his flesh he did not have the power to stand against his own sin nature.

When the Holy Spirit came, however, and he was regenerated, he was *endued with the power of God*, to not only stand strong for the name of Christ, but to give his life as he had once claimed he would. He proclaimed the gospel of Jesus Christ with power and boldness.

We are now freed not only to *not* do the things we hate but are enabled to *do* the things we should! We are freed by the Spirit to now "Mortify therefore" our "members which are upon the earth; fornication, uncleanness, inordinate affection, evil concupiscence, and covetousness, which is idolatry: For which things' sake the wrath of God cometh on the children of disobedience: In the which ye also walked some time, *when ye lived in them...*" and to "put off all these; anger, wrath, malice, blasphemy, filthy communication out of your mouth. Lie not one to another, seeing that *ye have put off* the old man with his deeds; And...*put on* the new man, which is renewed in knowledge after the image of him that created him: (Colossians 3:5-10)

We are to reckon ourselves dead to sin and alive unto God through Christ our Lord. Salvation through Christ conquered sin's power and condemnation of death by the law, making us dead to sin. We are no longer bound as servants to sin, but able to be servants of God.

I personally relate so much to Paul's testimony here. When I was a false convert, living in sin, I'm so thankful that a godly Christian cared enough to tell me that my sinful lifestyle was not pleasing to God and that I needed to repent, even addressing my known sins by name.

It wasn't easy to hear, and I even lied and denied some of it; but the Holy Spirit convicted me greatly through it. I knew that I did indeed need to turn from my sin and to God.

I tried my best to stop doing the things that I was convicted of, but it seemed the more I tried, the more I failed. I found that I could not be what I wanted to be. If I stopped one sin, I became aware of another. Repentance (like obedience to the law) could not save me from my sin, because sin was ever present in me. This process however was an essential part of showing me my need for a Savior and turning me from the path of sin.

The trying and failing to get rid of my sin convinced me of my unrighteousness and of God's righteous judgment against me. Like Paul, I knew that I needed deliverance from this body of death. Not that I could have stated it in those words at the time, but my helplessness showed me that I needed to be saved from my sin.

> "O wretched man that I am! who shall deliver me from the body of this death?" (Romans 7:24)

This was the preparation of my heart to receive the gospel of Jesus Christ, the only one who could deliver me from sin. Sadly, many today have never known this struggle with sin because modern Christianity refuses to address sin and the need for repentance but preaches *only accept Jesus*. Many of our converts have *asked Jesus into their hearts* with no desire to turn from sin, or to be reconciled to God.

Others who grew up in church and accepted Jesus at a young age, may conform outwardly to the social demands of the church community, but have never truly come to the knowledge of their own sinfulness. I have even heard some claim that since they were saved at a young age, they never really got into sin, so there was not much to repent of, hence no real change.

That genuinely alarms me when I hear such things! Paul, a Pharisee who desired to please God and served him zealously, even persecuting those whom he believed were against God, had to come to a knowledge of his own sin.

Through his desire to obey the law, he saw his sinfulness and inability to do so. This proved to him that the law was holy and just and good, while he himself was not. That which he thought would make him righteous before God only served to prove his unrighteousness.

> "Wherefore the law is holy, and the commandment holy, and just, and good. Was then that which is good made death unto me? God forbid. But sin, that it might appear sin, working death in me by that which is good; that sin by the commandment might become exceeding sinful." (Romans 7:12-13)

Paul, this Pharisee, and son of a Pharisee who sat at the

feet of Gamaliel *was radically changed* by salvation in Christ. Why should we expect anything less for our children or our converts? Can we possibly suggest that their righteousness exceeds that of the Pharisees?

Is it any wonder that we have so many even within the church that are enslaved to sin? Those who have never known the depths of their sin and the struggled to repent of it, cannot possibly understand the freedom from sin found in salvation through Christ.

> "Knowing this, that our old man is crucified with him, that the body of sin might be destroyed, that **henceforth we should not serve sin**. For he that is dead **is freed from sin**." (Romans 6:6-7)

Today we use Paul's testimony, not to proclaim freedom from sin's power over us, but to excuse the never-ending struggle of sin's captivity. We act as though this is all part of the normal Christian life. Paul was saying the very opposite.

Paul's message was not a sad account of his struggles, but a message of deliverance and power and praise to God!

As born-again believers, sin still dwells within our flesh, but it should not characterize our lives. If our hearts are truly seeking to glorify God, sin should be the exception, not the rule of our lives.

If you have the indwelling Holy Spirit of God, then according to the word of God, sin has no dominion over you. Can I suggest that if you are still enslaved to sin, *something is very wrong*? Quite possibly, you have not been made free (you are not saved).

Now, if you think that you can, as a Christian, continue as a servant of sin, comforting yourself that at least you are saved; think again. This is a very dangerous place to be. God will not allow his child to live a life of blatant, unrepentant sin without chastening you.

If you can continue in sin without chastening, it only *proves* that you are not his child. The true child of God does not want to continue in sin; but rejoices in that he has been made free.

> "Let not sin therefore reign in your mortal body, that ye should obey it in the lusts thereof. Neither yield ye your members as instruments of unrighteousness unto sin: but yield yourselves unto God, as those that are alive from the dead, and your members as instruments of righteousness unto God." (Romans 6:12-13)

Through salvation we *can* serve God in righteousness and in holiness! Oh, dear Christian walk in the Spirit and in the freedom from sin!

CHAPTER 6
THE BEGINNING OF WISDOM

When it comes to evangelism, even serious Bible students sometimes fail to see the big picture. Many Christians act as though the Old Testament is irrelevant for today because we are in the age of grace. Because of this, they focus most of their studies in the New Testament alone.

There is a tremendous danger in attempting to interpret the New Testament apart from the Old. I believe that we have done exactly that with our misinterpretation of Romans chapter ten.

We have applied our wrong ideas about how salvation is *received*, to all our evangelism, minimizing the gospel and seeking after professions at any cost. Modern evangelism has ignored the vital truths about repentance and genuine belief in God shown throughout the Old Testament.

The Old Testament was written for our example, it pictures for us, not only how to come to salvation, but also how to lead others to Christ as well.

"Search the Scriptures; for in them ye think ye have eternal life: and they are they which testify of me." (John 5:39)

What is the beginning of wisdom? The fear of the Lord. Over and over we read that phrase, *the fear of the Lord*. It seems like that may be a good place to start.

"The fear of the LORD is the beginning of wisdom: and the knowledge of the holy is understanding." (Proverbs 9:10)

"My son, if thou wilt receive my words, and hide my commandments with thee; So that thou incline thine ear unto wisdom, and apply thine heart to understanding; Yea, if thou criest after knowledge, and liftest up thy voice for understanding; If thou seekest her as silver, and searchest for her as for hid treasures; **Then** shalt thou understand the fear of the LORD, and find the knowledge of God." (Proverbs 2:1-5)

The fear of the Lord comes from a correct understanding of who God is and what he desires from us.

Only when we see the righteousness of God and his just condemnation of our sin can we appreciate the sacrifice he has provided for our sin. Just as only they that are sick need a physician; only they that see their need to be saved, can embrace the Savior.

How do we develop a fear of the Lord? By a knowledge of God's perfect standard of righteousness and by seeing how far short we fall from it because of sin. That is why the law is the schoolmaster to bring us to faith; because "…by the law is the knowledge of sin." (Romans 3:20)

"… I had not known sin, but by the law: for I had not known lust, except the law had said, Thou shalt not covet." (Romans 7:7)

In order to teach the fear of the Lord we must first teach who God is, and what his righteous commands for us are. Who is this God that he should be feared? God is holy, and good, merciful and compassionate. He knows all and sees all and is everywhere all the time. He is terrible, all powerful, righteous and just in judgment. He is the God of the Old Testament as well as the New. He is the same now as he ever was. He does not change. Only when the lost know who he is, can they truly revere him, and desire to be reconciled to him.

> "Wherefore the law was our schoolmaster to bring us unto Christ, that we might be justified by faith." (Galatians 3:24)

Through learning his laws, they begin to see his holiness in contrast to their own sin. The trying and failing to keep the law proves their unrighteousness in contrast to God's righteousness according to the law. By learning of his righteous judgment of the wicked, they recognize their own sin and need for a Savior. In seeing God's great mercy and provision, they see his great love for man and recognize his great grace and unspeakable gift.

I know that many of you are saying, "but we are not under the law." It is true that we that are saved are no longer under the condemnation of the law; but those who are not saved are yet condemned by the law.

> "For when the Gentiles, which have not the law, do by nature the things contained in the law, these, having not the law, are a law unto themselves: Which shew the work of the law **written in their hearts**, their conscience also bearing witness, and their thoughts the mean while accusing or else excusing one another;" (Romans 2:14-15)

Even we as Gentiles, who were not given the law are condemned by our own consciences when we go against the things contained in the law, our consciences become a law against us. The law is *not* the *way of righteousness*, it is the *revealer of unrighteousness*. Through the teaching of the law, we learn how righteous and holy our great God is and how far short we come of his glory.

Modern evangelism, however, begins *not* with the *fear of the Lord*, but with the offer of heaven to those

who, quite frankly, are not completely convinced they deserve hell.

Most of these efforts are geared toward children, often just out of the nursery, who have no fear of the Lord. They know nothing of God, sin, or of their need for repentance. Most barely know their right hand from their left. Yet, we do all we can to convince them that they are ready to be accountable for their sin before our holy God and responsible for their eternal destination.

Children are, in general, very receptive to our offer of a free ticket to heaven (and some candy) in return for a prayer. Who wouldn't raise their hand for this? We convince them to make decisions for Christ, and then send them home to evangelize their parents. Sounds great, right?

Child Evangelism

Although this book primarily addresses adult evangelism; since children's ministries have become the biggest outreach of the modern church, (essentially eliminating soul winning) I would be amiss to skip over the issues of child evangelism.

Let me begin by saying that I absolutely believe in teaching children, training them in the way which they should go. I also believe that if we have opportunity to witness to unchurched children, we should do our utmost to plant seeds and to educate them with as much information about God and his marvelous plan of salvation as we can. I am not against children's ministries; but *how* we minister to these children *must be biblical*.

The modern push to get children *to accept Jesus* as early as possible certainly came from the very best of intentions. We sincerely believed that getting all these kids to *make decisions for the Lord* would make a great difference in their futures and in the futures of our towns; but we must now admit that it has not worked as we hoped.

At one time, I went to a church that very zealously evangelized children through their Bible clubs. Almost every door in that town is now answered by someone who claims to have been saved as a child, through that ministry. The evidences however do not support those claims. These now adult children, who were convinced to say a prayer and told that they were saved; live in drug addiction, fornication and alcohol abuse, just the same as the unsaved.

When these *saved* kids finally reached the age where they could remove themselves from parental authority, the very first decision they made as adults (now consciously accountable to God) was to leave church and turn their backs on God.

It seems to be the same story in every church today. Yet despite our obvious lack of genuine fruits, we continue to celebrate our great and glorious victories every time we lead one of these little ones through a prayer. We ignore the truth, that these children who often seem so sincere in our Bible clubs and Sunday school classes, that sing songs and recite verses, reach adulthood and decide that they do not want anything to do with church or God.

Why do they go off and live in sin and wicked rebellion against God?

> "The transgression of the wicked saith within my heart, that **there is no fear of God before his eyes**." (Psalms 36:1)

The Bible tells us that the wicked do wickedly because there is *no fear of the Lord*. They have no genuine reverence for God. They, like Pharaoh ask, "Who is the LORD, that I should obey his voice...?" (Exodus 5:2) They do not obey God because they do not *really* believe God.

What could be the reason these twenty-something year old's, who at one time made decisions to follow the Lord, make such a radical departure from the faith? Not only were they *not* taught the fear of the Lord, but they were not mature enough to make such decisions in the first place. Their brains were quite simply not developed enough to accommodate such decisions.

If a four, five, or even a ten-year-old decided to commit their lives to becoming an astronaut or a ballerina, would we honestly expect that to be a binding commitment? No, of course we wouldn't; but we regularly convince these little ones to commit their lives to following Christ and act as though that same immature decision *is* a binding commitment. Or, worse yet, we make no mention of following Christ and simply offer Heaven in exchange for a prayer.

Underdeveloped Prefrontal Cortex

Science has proven that a child's brain is not fully developed until they are in their mid-twenties. The last area to fully mature is the Prefrontal Cortex, the area of the brain known as the executive center. This area is responsible for coordinating complex cognitive functions such as reasoning, behavioral control, attentional control, planning and understanding the consequences of decisions as well as inhibiting poor choices.

The ability to differentiate between conflicting thoughts, determine what is good and bad, understand future consequences of current activities, work toward desired goals, and apply behavioral controls (suppressing urges with the possibility of socially unacceptable outcomes) all rely on executive function.

Simply being able to plan and follow through on long term goals is dependent upon simultaneous use of these executive functions. The Prefrontal Cortex which controls these functions is simply not developed enough until after twenty years of age to consistently perform in this way. I don't think it is any coincidence that this is the age where many of the kids we have claimed for Christ *turn from God.*

Until the Prefrontal Cortex is developed, their decision

making is handled primarily by the Amygdala, the same place that processes the fight or flight response. It is the seat of their emotions. Children are quite simply *governed* by their emotions. That's why they are fickle and easily tossed about. One day they are cooperative and happy, and the next, they are defiant and inconsolably depressed because of something that to us, would seem insignificant.

The connections are still developing between their emotional and rational thinking. Being able to process and regulate their emotions in order to formulate a logical response is basically beyond their ability. That is why it is necessary for us to continually teach them principles for behavior and appropriate responses that they then practice throughout their childhood.

We teach them how to behave and think and train them to work toward goals and help them to learn through our encouragement, to follow through. We guide them to apply these principles that they will one day use for themselves, because we know that, as children, they cannot yet do this on their own.

Even society in general, recognizes the limitations of a child. We do not allow children to drink until they are twenty-one. They cannot vote and serve in the military until age eighteen. Eighteen, by the way, is the perfect age for military service because on the outside, they have the capabilities of adults, but inside they are children with brains that are still developing. They have not yet experienced the inhibitions that come from age, or the logic and the understanding of consequences that comes with experience; and so, they are still quite fearless.

When these children and teens commit crimes, they are even prosecuted differently, because we know that they are not responsible for their own decisions. Their brains are just not developed enough to make mature decisions. *[margin note: not true]*

We all know well, the impulsivity of children and their limitations intellectually, and yet in the church, we make a regular practice of pressing children and teens to make life decisions that they are not yet prepared to make and insist that they trust in these moments of decision for their eternal destinations.

We take the teens (who are honestly only interested in socializing with the opposites sex) to camps and youth conventions where they run on candy, games, pizza, and sleep deprivation. Many of these are unchurched kids who have not been taught the fear of the Lord, or his righteousness. Then in an emotion filled plea, we try to make them understand the consequences of their sin and Christ's substitutionary death on the cross and counsel them to plan for their eternal destinations. We secure decisions from them and breathe a big sigh of relief as though our work is done.

We believe that these wonderful, and exciting experiences will enable them to more easily embrace Christ, but in fact, heightened emotions work *against* rational decision making. When the emotions are excited, they basically highjack the decision-making. Any sparking connections to the Prefrontal Cortex are diverted and the emotions take over. They are no longer processing decisions but acting on their emotions.

Not only does the brain *not* respond rationally to fleshly excitement; but appealing to their flesh also does *not* produce a spiritual outcome; for we know that the flesh and the Spirit are contrary one to another.

> "For the flesh lusteth against the Spirit, and the Spirit against the flesh: and these are contrary the one to the other: ..." (Galatians 5:17)

With smaller children, we stir them up with games, prizes, puppets and exciting stories. Although we are aware that many still struggle with what's real and what's not, we take advantage of their vivid imaginations and the fact that they are just as willing to believe in Christ, as they are to believe in fairies and unicorns, and call it child-like faith.

Child-*ish* faith is not the same as child-*like* faith.

The Bible tells us that we are not to be childish in our understanding. Faith is trusting in the revealed truth of God. There must be an understanding of salvation.

Believing the facts of Jesus' death, burial and resurrection is not the same as believing in Jesus for salvation. Jesus came to call *sinners* to repentance. A child must be capable of understanding that they are sinners before our holy God and repenting. This requires a certain level of comprehension.

Child-like faith means trusting completely without reservation, not merely a fleeting emotional response. Unless a child understands his sin against God, and his just condemnation, (which requires an understanding of consequences) he cannot understand his *need* for a Savior.

Even still, we encourage them to make professions, lead them through prayers and send them home as though they are prepared for eternity. Then we wonder why all these kids we *led to the Lord* do not follow through with those decisions when they are older. We wonder why they depart from the faith.

I realize that many people have their own or their child's experience, so engrained in their minds that it may be hard to view this from a purely *biblical perspective*; but if our experiences do not line up with Scripture, we must reject them and stand on the truth. Please try, as far as you are able, to put aside opinions and experiences and evaluate our practices *by God's word alone*.

They leave us, and go out into the world to secular colleges, or the workforce and find that, the cost of following Christ is much higher than they thought. In their yet unregenerate minds, the wisdom of the world begins to make much more sense than what we have taught them. Many like Eve, even begin to think that God was withholding this wisdom from them. Often, they feel deceived and foolish for having believed our views.

They *have tried* our Jesus and *our magic prayer* and *found them wanting*. They did not experience the new life, or freedom from the power of sin, or spiritual understanding we promised them. When they finally get to the point where they are convicted of their sin and see the error of their ways, what is left to offer if we've already convinced them that they are saved? What salvation is left for them then?

We have to some extent, taken away any hope of salvation for them by convincing them that they already tried it. The truth is, we have left many of them in worse condition than when we found them!

> "For if after they have escaped the pollutions of the world through the knowledge of the Lord and Saviour Jesus Christ, they are again entangled therein, and overcome, the latter end is worse with them than the beginning. **For it had been better for them not to have known the way of righteousness, than, after they have known it, to turn from the holy commandment delivered unto them.** But it is happened unto them according to the true proverb, The dog is turned to his own vomit again; and the sow that was washed to her wallowing in the mire." (2 Peter 2:20-22)

We make excuses for them, call them *carnal* Christians and pray that they will someday return, because we refuse to see the truth. We have encouraged them to make decisions that they were not capable of making. Their brains were simply not yet prepared to process long term decisions, because they could not yet logically even reason through the consequences of their actions. The very few who do *return*, struggle with the guilt and shame of having gone off into sin.

Until they become adults, not only do they *not* have the capability to make life choices, they do *not* have the freedom.

They are not yet self-governing, so even if they choose to live for Christ as children, we cannot know the reality of that choice until they are much older.

Children may have *moments* of what seems to be a sincere desire to love and obey the Lord. They may seem to believe the facts that we tell them *about* Jesus and *about* sin and Hell; but that does not mean that are repentant toward God regarding *their* sin and trusting in Christ for their salvation.

The ability to follow through on their commitment to follow Christ is just beyond their grasp. These same children who desire to be fishers of men today, choose tomorrow to be firemen or policemen.

It is not until adulthood that they for the first time, have the power and the ability to govern their own lives. Only then are they making the very first decisions that they have ever been able to make. This is the true *test* of their professed faith. Will they follow Christ and live the faith they claimed or walk away? Faith that has not been tested is not faith. If their faith does not have works, it is dead. The truest evidence of genuine faith is obedience to God.

Many people expect kids to *backslide* when they become teenagers, but if when they become old enough to self-govern, they have the indwelling Holy Spirit, wouldn't we expect to see them yielding to that rather than being overcome of the flesh? According to the Bible we should.

> "For they that are after the flesh do mind the things of the flesh; but they that are after the Spirit the things of the Spirit." (Romans 8:5)

Falling away is simply evidence of *unbelief* at *any age*. Why is it so hard for us to see that if they abandon the faith, they were simply not saved?

Let me be clear before we go any further. I'm *not* saying that children *cannot* be saved until after their Prefrontal Cortex is developed. God can, of course, do anything including saving a child at a young age. There may very well be children with spiritual knowledge and understanding beyond their years; but I believe it is probably the exception rather than the rule.

In today's Christianity, we have come to *expect* children to be saved at a young age. Instead of striving for more teaching and biblical training, we now strive to obtain decisions earlier and earlier. These decisions, however, are just not an accurate representation of genuine salvations.

Are Science and Christianity compatible?

Now, you may be thinking that this scientific perspective is irrelevant or incompatible with faith and Christianity, but as a matter of fact, the Bible supports this scientific information very well.

In the book of Deuteronomy, we see God punishing the sins of the Israelites, but telling them that he would not hold their children accountable *who did not yet know good and evil.*

> "Moreover your little ones, which ye said should be a prey, and your children, which in that day had no Knowledge between good and evil, they shall go in thither, and unto them will I give it, and they shall possess it" (Deuteronomy 1:39).

How old were these children that God said did not yet know good and evil and would not be held accountable? All that were under twenty years old. God calls them *little ones.*

This is very significant. God did not say that these children did not know any better in this isolated situation. He said that they just plain did not yet know good from evil.

I know that this is not how we see children today; but unless we were to suggest that this specific group was uncharacteristically slow-minded; we would have to admit that this is how God sees children of this age.

In this very familiar account, the children of Israel have sent men to spy out the land that God has promised them.

Two followed God wholly and gave report of the blessings awaiting them in the land. The other ten, however, came back fearful and murmuring against God, not believing God would see them safely into the land. They feared for their wives and children and would not follow the Lord's commands.

The Lord told them that because of their unbelief, the adults would not enter into the promised land, but their children whom they did not trust God to protect, would. God would *not hold these children accountable* for the sin of unbelief, but all the rest of the people (the adults) would be held accountable.

> "Your carcasses shall fall in this wilderness; and all that were numbered of you, according to your whole number, from twenty years old and upward, which have murmured against me, Doubtless ye shall not come into the land, concerning which I sware to make you dwell therein, save Caleb the son of Jephunneh, and Joshua the son of Nun. **But your little ones, which ye said should be a prey, them will I bring in,** and they shall know the land which ye have despised. But as for you, your carcasses, they shall fall in this wilderness. And your children shall wander in the wilderness forty years, and bear your whoredoms, until your carcasses be wasted in the wilderness." (Numbers 14:29-33)

Twenty years old is a very different age than the age we are attempting to make children accountable today.

We see this event recounted again with the age of twenty being the determination of accountability in Numbers 32:11 "Surely none of the men that came up out of Egypt, **from twenty years old and upward,** shall see the land which I sware unto Abraham, unto Isaac, and unto Jacob; because they have not wholly followed me".

Twenty is also the age a man was counted in census and was also able to go to war.

"**From twenty years old and upward**, all that are able to go forth to war in Israel: thou and Aaron shall number them by their armies" (Numbers 1:3)

It is even more interesting that at age twenty, the age when a man was recognized as numbered among the people, he was also then required to offer tribute for his own soul.

"Every one that passeth among them that are numbered, from twenty years old and above, shall give an offering unto the LORD" (Exodus 30:14).

Jamieson, Fausset and Brown Bible commentary: This was not a voluntary contribution, but a ransom for the soul or lives of the people. It was required from all classes alike, and a refusal to pay implied a wilful exclusion from the privileges of the sanctuary, as well as exposure to divine judgments. ("Commentary on Exodus 30 by Jamieson, Fausset & Brown. 1871" Blue Letter Bible. Last modified 19 Feb, 2000.)

So, does this prove that the age of accountability is twenty? *No, of course not.* It would be foolish to be so dogmatic. It *does* however offer support for the doctrine of the age of accountability.

Because there are *no accounts* of children being saved or baptized, or even being evangelized in the Scriptures, *we do not have any* concrete examples to form our doctrine of a child's age of accountability before God or the appropriate age for evangelism. This has led to speculations and debate throughout history.

This often-overlooked account that we have just looked at, clearly establishes that link between understanding and accountability/imputation of sin. It is perhaps one of the only Scriptures from which we can even possibly establish any precept regarding age of accountability. God tells us that all that were under twenty *did not know good from evil* and so, would not be held accountable.

If we are going to be biblical or even logical, we would certainly have to admit that there is, *at the very least*, a definite possibility that the children we spend so much time and effort attempting to lead to a decision are not yet even accountable to God because of their lack of understanding.

If it is possible that accountability has not yet been established, or sin imputed to their account, how do we think that they can be saved? *What exactly are they saved from* if, they do not yet know good from evil and so, are not yet accountable?

Teaching children to fear the Lord is clearly appropriate at any age; and training up a child most certainly should begin as early as possible. Declaring a child (of any age) to be already saved, however, is presumptuous at best.

Could this be why we do not see any examples of child evangelism in the Scriptures?

What we see in the Scriptures is admonitions for parents to train *their* children, and for children to obey their parents, (not lead their parents to the Lord). In modern Christianity, however, seeking after children to evangelize has become the most important outreach of the church. If child evangelism was truly intended to be the primary avenue to spread the gospel, wouldn't there be biblical examples for us to follow?

Where are the stories of the Apostles seeking after the children of Jerusalem, Samaria or the utter-most parts of the earth? Where are the stories of children being baptized after Peter preached at VBS or AWANA? Where are the commands to teach faithful children, that shall be able to teach their parents also?

Do we honestly believe that God somehow failed to foresee the need today to reach families through their children? Could we even suggest that God's instructions to us were incomplete?

We do not see the disciples running children's ministries or gathering the children from unbelieving homes to evangelize. *What we see them witnessing to men and women.* They did not forbid children to come along and to be blessed by Christ; but *nowhere do we see them preaching to children* and *calling for children to decide* their eternal destinations.

There are *no* written accounts of children being saved or baptized in the Scriptures.

Instead, what we see is Jesus and the Disciples focusing their efforts on adults. Why? Because they were commanded to teach faithful men who would be able to teach others also. Believing parents were commanded to train up *their own* children in the faith.

Recent studies have shown that when the Father of a family gets saved first, on average, there is a 93% chance that the rest of the family will get saved as well. When the Mother gets saved first, it drops down to a mere 17% chance. But get this, when a child is the first to get saved, there is only 3.5% chance that the rest of the family will get saved as a result. *Why* then are we attempting to reach families through the children?

According to an article by S. Michael Craven published by the Christian Post, Studies show that the salvation of Fathers is far more important than we ever realized.

> "In short, if a father does not go to church-no matter how faithful his wife's devotions-only one child in 50 will become a regular worshipper. If a father does go regularly, regardless of the practice of the mother, between two-thirds and three-quarters of their children will become churchgoers (regular and irregular). One of the reasons suggested for this distinction is that children tend to take their cues about domestic life from Mom while their conceptions of the world outside come from Dad. If Dad takes faith in God seriously then the message to their children is that God should be taken

seriously.

This confirms the essential role of father as spiritual leader, which I would argue is true fatherhood. Fathers are to love their wives as Christ loves the church, modeling the love of the Father in their most important earthly relationship. Fathers are to care for their children as our Father in heaven cares for us and finally, fathers play a primary role in teaching their children the truth about reality." (Fathers, Key to Their Children's Faith by S. Michael Craven Christian Post Guest Contributor)

Clearly *God's way* of evangelizing families is far more effective than *ours*. Could this be why child evangelism was *not* practiced by the Disciples, or the early church? These ministries are modern traditions, not founded on biblical commands or examples. Sunday school, which first began around 1751, was originally developed to teach underprivileged children to read and write; but was very quickly adopted by the church.

Sunday school and bus ministries have long since been employed as church growth methods. It is thought that if we can lure the children in, then the parents will follow. Not only is this *not* effective evangelism, as we have already seen; but if we are disregarding God's command to go and evangelize men and women, substituting these children's programs instead, we are quite simply disobedient! We are, according to the Bible, to *train our children and to evangelize adults*. It's as simple as that.

I realize that the statement I am about to make is not one that is easy to receive, but I have come to the place, through much study and prayer, where I sincerely believe that our over-emphasis on children's ministries is in fact a distraction of the Devil.

If there were one thing that the Devil could use to turn our hearts from saving the souls of the lost, what would it be? What would make us abandon our commission to go and preach the gospel to lost men and women? *Children!* God's word is clear that we are to go and preach the gospel to every creature, and while that may include children, it certainly does not mean to the exclusion of adults.

Children's ministries in modern Christianity have done exactly that by taking the place of adult evangelism. Those who are zealous for the Lord and desire to see souls saved have sadly, been convinced that evangelism is best accomplished through children's ministries. This is simply not true. I know that this idea is a hard pill for most to swallow and is certainly not going to make me popular with anyone, but the truth never has been popular.

God tells us to train up a child.

Let me say emphatically again, that I am not against corporately teaching children within the church. Believe me, as a parent, I need all the godly support and assistance I can get in training my child. Teaching a child at *every opportunity*, to live for God, to obey and worship him, telling them about his grace and mercy shown to us through his precious plan of salvation absolutely is biblical.

Pressing children to make decisions that they are then counselled to trust for their eternal salvations is, in my opinion, absurd.

Many seem to believe that as long as a child claims to *believe* at the moment of their profession, then they are saved, no matter what they do later in life. So then, when they go off into the world and live in sin, they insist that at least they are going to Heaven.

This type of thinking surpasses even the magic prayer mentality in its disregard of Bible truth. The greatest evidence of genuine saving faith is *continuation*, *not* merely a fleeting moment of belief from a child. It is not a temporary interest in pleasing God; but a life of reconciliation to God.

Saving faith is an enduring trust in Christ not just a moment of belief. A child can easily believe in what he knows about God and Jesus, but when it comes time for them to decide who will be *their* God, that is where the rubber meets the road. They can believe all the things we tell them and profess to even love Jesus, but if they are not willing to obey him, then according to the Scriptures, they are liars.

> "He that saith, I know him, and keepeth not his commandments, is a liar, and the truth is not in him." (1 John 2:4)

That is why training up a child requires so much more than simply coercing a decision from an emotional preschooler or adolescent. Just because a child claims to understand and agree or even parrots back what we have said, does not mean that it has taken root in their heart or even in their mind.

When my kids were little, I taught them about looking both ways before crossing the street. They could recite the rule frontwards and backwards; and yet, at the first opportunity, they each chased a ball into the street without looking. It had not yet become something they could apply for themselves. That is why we need to continue teaching our children diligently and consistently.

> "And thou shalt love the LORD thy God with all thine heart, and with all thy soul, and with all thy might. And these words, which I command thee this day, shall be in thine heart: **And thou shalt teach them diligently unto thy children,** and shalt **talk of them when thou sittest in thine house**, and **when thou walkest by the way,** and **when thou liest down**, and **when thou risest up**. And thou shalt bind them for a sign upon thine hand, and they shall be as frontlets between thine eyes. And thou shalt write them upon the posts of thy house, and on thy gates." (Deuteronomy 6:5-9)

The word diligently means, constantly or continually,

with effort to accomplish the desired goal. That's not calling for a decision after one brief lesson, but a lot of training!

Spiritual training helps to give them the tools they need.

Memorizing Scriptures and learning spiritual principles even aides in the development of their brains by encouraging connections to the Prefrontal Cortex. While offering exciting fun and games may be more appealing, it is of little benefit.

The power of the word of God spiritually working in the heart, coupled with the preaching/teaching of the word stirs the soul as well as the intellect, challenging them to think and encouraging brain development. This is the heart of training. That is why we need to *stop manipulating emotions, stop collecting their decisions*, and *start teaching as much Scripture and wisdom from God's word as possible.*

A child needs this continuing training, not just one-time teaching because his brain grows in spurts. As it grows, it develops connections and stores new information, and at times, eliminates some of what was there previously. What is learned at one point may need to be retaught later. Training is repeating a lesson or practice until it becomes a governing principle.

Children may have a knowledge of what to do, but their feelings will trump that knowledge every time. It takes time and work. Ask anyone who has raised kids, how many years it took to train their children to brush their teeth after every meal.

Learning to apply the things we teach them such as brushing, eating right, going to church, and even following the Lord does not happen in a day. Any parent can tell you that what their child or teen happily agrees to today, they might just as easily refuse tomorrow. If we trained children up in tooth brushing the way we evangelize them, they would have no teeth left by adulthood!

Training is teaching them to do the right thing, rewarding good behavior and disciplining poor behavior *until* behaving the right way becomes their normal behavior. It doesn't happen overnight. There *will be* set-backs, growth, regression, just as with a baby's sleep training. Just because it works today, does not mean your training is done.

I remember at one time, thinking that some of the lessons I was trying to teach were not working because my kids continued to do the things that they had been disciplined for over and over. It was not that the training was ineffective, but simply that it needed to be continued consistently, *until* it accomplished the desired effect.

That is why God gave children parents, to teach them and to protect them from their own unwise decisions *until* these lessons take hold of their hearts. We, as parents act as their external controls until they are mature enough to use their own internal controls. *We* make the hard choices for them and enforce them when necessary, because we can see the consequences to their actions. *We* can logically assess a situation and make the appropriate judgment and even follow through on them for the long term, *while our child cannot*.

We make these decisions and exercise that control over them for as long as we can. Then, when they will no longer submit to our authority, we let go and pray that their own internal restraints are developed, and function as they should according to what we have taught them.

We train them to live and act and think in obedience to God so that they will be in the habit of living that way. Obedience will become their way of life and anything else will seem strange. We train them by not only our parental influence of speaking and living the word, but also by surrounding them with others who also walk by faith.

Then, when the decision-making place within their brains finally do begin to govern their choices, they can draw from the information they have, to make right decisions. They will, hopefully, be equipped to withstand the assault of secular humanism that they will face in the world. If we have trained them properly, they should be fully equipped and ready to make right decisions.

Obviously, they still have a free will and can choose wrong if that is their desire, but we pray that they will choose to live for God even when we are no longer making that decision for them.

For the children who come from unbelieving homes, training to be a follower of the Lord is nonexistent. The training they receive at home is how to live life apart from God. Every day of their lives, they are learning some form of humanism from godless parents seeking after the lusts of the flesh and the lust of the eyes as well as the pride of life. They are learning self-esteem, not God esteem.

Worshipping God does not come naturally for a child, because, from a child's perspective, the world revolves around him.

He does not understand that they are made to glorify God. They cannot possibly understand denying themselves and taking up their cross.

Anyone who has children has seen the pure, unrestrained selfishness of a child's heart. *Their* needs and desires are all that they can see. According to God, they do not yet understand good and evil. They only know what *they* want. That is why it is necessary for us to teach them what is a good and acceptable way to express their desires and which desires are sinful and must be controlled. If they *do not even know right from wrong,* how do we really think they can repent of their sin?

When we do have opportunities to impact the lives of unchurched kids, we need to use these times to plant, and water the seed of the word instead of merely pressing them to make decisions. We cannot possibly *train up* the children that we bring in the way a saved parent would train their own, but we *can* introduce them to God and teach them his laws, *the schoolmaster that will one day lead them to faith.*

Yes, we should try to reach them, teaching them everything we can about God and his righteous standard. We should instruct them in his laws and his holiness. We should give them everything we possibly can in the way of biblical education; but what we most urgently need to do is *stop leading them through prayers* and then *giving them false assurances.*

I find it ironic that most churches that evangelize toddlers and preschoolers are reluctant to baptize them, and generally counsel their parents to wait. They call on these little ones to make decisions for their eternal destinations and pronounce them saved; but then do not even trust their professions enough to baptize them!

Why? Because they know that there must be genuine saving faith involved, naturally they question the reality of that faith at such young ages. Certainly, none would want to be viewed as those who superstitiously baptize babies, so they attempt to be more careful about their baptisms than about their salvations. How does this even make sense? If we are pronouncing toddlers and preschoolers saved, then how *are* we any better?

So then, should we withhold the gospel? Certainly not! What we need to withhold is our own false gospel of *just say this prayer*, as well as our false assurances.

We *should* preach the gospel, God's plan of reconciliation, so that they can see his love and great mercy toward them; but expecting these unlearned, immature children to be able to hold to lasting decisions to follow Christ is simply unrealistic, and often spiritually detrimental.

Our goal should be to train them in spiritual things, not merely to convince them to make decisions for Christ and call it done. Let them be the ones to tell us that they believe and trust Christ. Let *them* testify with their mouths and with their lives of their salvation, the same as we should expect from adults.

Biblical Children's Ministries

Why is it that Jehovah's witnesses, Muslims and other such false religions are so successful in raising committed, zealous followers? Why is it that their children learn chapters of their religious books while we struggle to teach ours verses from the Bible?

Is it because their games and activities are more fun than ours? Of course not. It is because they take training their children *seriously*. Now, that is not to hold them as a positive example in what they are teaching, but only that they are *diligently* teaching their children.

If we were serious about their training, children's church would be *practice for grown up church*. We would be training them to listen to age-appropriate preaching, challenging them to apply the teaching of the Bible, helping them to learn to live for God, assisting them in following along in their Bibles, and teaching them about tithing and serving in preparation to worship as we worship; but we are not.

We are training children to expect fun, games, prizes, and snacks. This is not training them to worship God the way we worship God. This is setting them up for failure and disappointment! We need to stop substituting entertainment for their spiritual training.

If you think that children are not capable of sitting still for an hour, it's only because we have not *expected* them to. If they are old enough to be in school, they certainly do it there. Children's ministries, if they are indeed ministries, should be about teaching them how to worship God, not merely how to be entertained and eat snacks.

It is a great privilege to be entrusted with the training of these precious souls for God. It is our job to represent our heavenly Father to them. *We are preparing them to love and obey their heavenly Father.* We should be teaching them how to one day behave like Christian adults.

We are a physical representation of God's authority to teach them how to obey him. Just as we read in Galatians, an heir answers to tutors and governors until the time appointed of the Father.

While we know that in this passage, these tutors and governors of course are a picture of the law, preparing us for faith, there is another very important lesson we can learn.

> "Now I say, That the heir, as long as he is a child, differeth nothing from a servant, though he be lord of all; But is under tutors and governors until the time appointed of the father" (Galatians 4:1-2).

That child, without proper training and maturity is simply not ready to accept the responsibility or accountability that goes along with being an heir. Therefore, he is under the authority of teachers, and those who will help to prepare him for that great responsibility. What age might that be? We cannot know. Only the Father knows that. That is why God gives children parents and teachers.

It is our job to ensure that they receive the best preparations humanly possible, so that they will be able to stand as a fitting representation of their heritage, strong enough to withstand the enemy. If we sent our own young child to these tutors and governors to be trained for such a time, and they sent him back home to us the same day, claiming that he is already prepared to answer for himself and to assume his rightful place; we would be furious!

We would never want our child to be robbed of the important lessons, or experiences necessary to teach him the truths he will need; but that is exactly what we do to the children that come through our children's ministries! We bring them in for a night, lead them through a prayer and then send them back to their parents, assuring them that their child is now prepared for eternity. How dare we?

When we do this, we are not planting good seed in their hearts but planting tares that will choke out any further seed that may be planted in the future.

We are removing any possible conviction of sin and need for repentance they may have by assuring them that their salvation has already been secured. We have honestly shirked our God-given responsibilities to these children. Why in the world would we try to shortchange a child on the spiritual training God has commanded us to give them? Why would we even want to pronounce them saved/accountable prematurely? -especially someone else's child? I would think that we would desire every single opportunity that God allows to prepare them to love and serve him and to teach them as much as we possibly can about his holiness and perfect standard of righteousness.

Wouldn't we want every moment to teach them of repentance and faith *before* they are responsible to answer to him on their own? Instead, we are in such a hurry to make them accountable to God, that we give them a bare bones gospel and run them through a sinner's prayer. Then we breathe a big sigh of relief and pat ourselves on the back as though our job is done. We should be ashamed!

We have not even come close to preparing these children for eternity. A simple mention of sin is often all we give. Most of the children we pronounce saved have *no idea what sin is*, other than an offense to Mom and Dad. *According to God, they do not understand good and evil* or that their actions are an offense to a holy and perfect God who demands our obedience.

Most often, those who profess Christ as a child, and *do* go on to live for him, are those that grew up in church. This, however, is *not* a testimony to child evangelism, but to proper training from faithful, believing parents. It testifies to God's wisdom in his plan for their spiritual training.

How many more generations of children will we lose? Modern Christianity has abandoned the doctrine of biblical repentance in our evangelism, and convinced children from the nursery up that they are already saved. Their *fear of the Lord* has essentially been *removed*.

As children, they already lack inhibition, self-control and

an understanding of the long-term consequences of their decisions. That is why kids who seemingly know better, make unwise and potentially destructive life decisions if given that freedom too early.

So often, these kids reach their teenage years and become so tempted by sin that they choose to turn away from God. This may be the first point in their lives that they have genuinely even struggled with sin.

Those who believe that they are already saved, may even indulge in sin more, with no knowledge of the danger of God's wrath. If we have convinced them that they are saved, then we have also removed any fear of the Lord that could have prompted their obedience. It's no wonder they are such easy targets of the Devil!

They often find themselves so deep in sin that they can't see a way out. The number of testimonies I have heard of professing teens attempting suicide is alarming to say the least!

I wonder how different it would be if they did not have false assurances. If they believed they were yet unsaved and in danger of God's wrath and of their own eternal destruction; would they be more guarded against it? Would they flee from it or at least fear it more?

How differently would we parent unsaved children and teens? How much more protective would we be? How much more training would we be giving them?

We cannot ignore the problem any longer!

We all know that our child evangelism efforts are not producing the results we desire. Even if we are unwilling to admit that these children are not saved, we cannot deny the fact that the majority do not live for Christ. Something is clearly wrong! I know it may seem easier to pretend that there is no problem than to face the enormity of the issue.

Trust me, it would be much easier for *me* personally to just get on board with Easy Believism and ride the child evangelism train with everyone else, than to stand alone.

It's not easy being viewed as a villain or a heretic because I dare point out that the magic prayer is not *really* magic. Calling sinners to repentance and faith and to be baptized as a testimony of their conversion, rather than merely reciting a prayer are almost scandalous ideas in the eyes of many Christians today. This should not be; but it is.

It's almost amusing that some have even questioned the motives for what I'm stating, accusing me of some sort of agenda, while those collecting quick decisions and big numbers are lauded for their efforts.

Please know and understand that it would be far easier to simply go along with the crowd, if the Lord would allow.

I have, in the past, taught Bible clubs and worked the exhaustingly exhilarating weeks of VBS and thrilled at the decisions made, right along with everyone else. These yearly outreach extravaganzas seem to grow bigger and more elaborate every year, along with the reports of *salvations*. The end of the week testimonies and accolades always seemed to create an emotional celebration, fueling a desire for even bigger numbers.

All that excitement and camaraderie are just plain hard to beat with biblical arguments or even logic. It is not easy to now stand alone and suggest that those decisions were more than likely not genuine.

I have prayed and prayed, asking God to correct me if I'm wrong, especially regarding child evangelism. I have humbled myself many times vowing to publicly confess my error and wholeheartedly embrace his truth if he showed me that what we are doing today is indeed biblical. Instead, he showed me even more that was wrong with what we are doing. I cannot in good conscience toward God turn a blind eye. *Can you?*

CHAPTER 7
SOWING THE INCORRUPTIBLE SEED

"... Go ye into all the world, and preach the gospel to every creature." (Mark 16:15)

What is the gospel? Most well-churched Christians, when asked this question, would immediately reference 1Corinthians 15:1-4.

"Moreover, brethren, I declare unto you the gospel which I preached unto you, which also ye have received, and wherein ye stand; By which also ye are saved, if ye keep in memory what I preached unto you, unless ye have believed in vain. For I delivered unto you first of all that which I also received, how that Christ died for our sins according to the Scriptures; And that he was buried, and that he rose again the third day according to the Scriptures" (1 Corinthians 15:1-4).

Of course, we know that this is the gospel, the good news of what our precious Savior Jesus Christ has done on behalf of sinful man. The death, burial and resurrection of Christ is the gospel in a nutshell. But, is this the whole message we are called to preach and teach?

Many Christians insist that since Paul did not mention repentance in this section of Scripture, that repentance is not part of the message we are called to preach. Why did Paul not mention repentance when he speaks of the gospel in 1 Corinthians chapter fifteen? Reading this passage of Scripture in its proper context, two points shed light on this question:

1. The Audience. Paul's letter to the Corinthians is obviously, a letter to a church, which means that he is speaking to believers. When preaching to those who claim to be believers, or Brethren, the message is often quite different than a message for unbelievers, or those whom you are seeking to evangelize. Quite simply, the reason Paul's letters to the churches did not specifically address repentance regarding salvation could be that he was addressing those who were already saved and had already come to repentance.

We do not see specific instructions for Evangelism or sermons to the unsaved recorded within these letters because they were written to the churches (believers). However, when we look at the book of Acts, which does tell us in detail what Paul preached, we see that Paul's message to the unsaved was clearly a message of repentance and faith.

> "Testifying both to the Jews, and also to the Greeks, **repentance toward God, and faith toward our Lord Jesus Christ**" (Acts 20:21)

> "Which when the apostles, Barnabas and Paul, heard of, they rent their clothes, and ran in among the people, crying out, And saying, Sirs, why do ye these things? We also are men of like passions with you, and **preach unto you that ye should turn from these vanities unto the living God,** which made heaven, and earth, and the sea, and all things that are therein" (Acts 14:14-15).

> "And the times of this ignorance God winked at; but **now commandeth all men every where to repent**" (Acts 17:30)

While that may seem to oversimplify the issue, I believe the next point answers the question a bit more specifically.

2. The Purpose. The book of First Corinthians was written by Paul to address various issues that had arisen within the church. He spends the first fourteen chapters addressing sin and error and establishing doctrine regarding questions raised, e.g.: division, carnality, fornication, going to law against one another, marital issues, the eating of meats offered to idols, liberties, and a rather large section on correcting misunderstanding regarding spiritual gifts, ending in chapter fourteen.

In chapter fifteen, he lays the groundwork to address yet another error that had begun to trouble the Church- the question of the resurrection of the dead. He sets forth the message of Christ's death, burial and resurrection, reminding them how that he has already taught them this, pointing out the eyewitnesses which testified to these. Then he goes on to ask:

> "Now if Christ be preached that he rose from the dead, how say some among you that there is no resurrection of the dead? But if there be no resurrection of the dead, then is Christ not risen" (1Corinthians 15:12-13).

He explains to them that without Christ's resurrection, his preaching would be in vain, and our faith would be pointless, for we would be without hope. When he describes the gospel in this passage, it is not to unbelievers for the purpose of evangelization, but to believers for the purpose of proving Christ's resurrection.

Paul's focus is on showing Christ's resurrection and why it is essential to believe it. His intent is to correct and instruct believers, it was not to evangelize the lost or to teach evangelism. He then goes on to teach of the rapture and deliverance of those who died already (which hinge upon the resurrection).

He finishes the letter with chapter sixteen which

discusses the collection for the saints and his closing thoughts. These are just two likely reasons Paul did not specifically mention repentance within this passage. Paul's gospel message did not change, dropping repentance as some would suggest.

The Gospel message preached by Paul and the apostles, to Jew and Gentile alike, has always included repentance toward God as well as faith toward Jesus Christ.

> "And how I kept back nothing that was profitable unto you, but have shewed you, and have taught you publickly, and from house to house, Testifying both to the Jews, and also to the Greeks, **repentance toward God, and faith toward our Lord Jesus Christ**" (Acts 20:20-21)

Paul tells us that he did not keep anything back. He gave them the whole counsel of God- "repentance toward God and faith toward our Lord and Savior Jesus Christ" (Acts 20:21). Paul's message always included repentance, as did the message of the other Apostles.

In the book of Acts, we read of Paul reasoning and disputing in the synagogue for days at a time. In chapter seventeen we see him preaching to the men of Athens. He did not simply give an ABC's, or one, two, three's gospel message; he preached to them the identity of God, who he is, his hand in creation & his personal relationship and availability to men.

He preached God's righteous judgment and the coming resurrection as well as the good news of Jesus Christ. Then when some said they would hear him again, and clung to him, he continued preaching to them. As a matter of fact, never did he lead anyone through a prayer or pronounce them saved, even if they were convicted. Instead, he simply instructed those who repented and believed to be baptized.

When Peter preached on the day of Pentecost, "they were pricked in their heart, and said unto Peter and to the rest of the apostles, Men and brethren, what shall we do?" (Acts 2:37). Why? Because Peter preached to them about their sin against God first, and how that they had rejected and crucified their long-awaited Savior that died to bring salvation to them.

> "Therefore let all the house of Israel know assuredly, that God hath made that same Jesus, whom ye have crucified, both Lord and Christ" (Acts 2:36).

In the horror of their realization they asked, "what shall we do?" (to take away their sins and be made right with God). Peter's answer certainly was not, repeat this prayer after me. Peter told them to repent and be baptized.

> "Then Peter said unto them, Repent, and be baptized every one of you in the name of Jesus Christ for the remission of sins, and ye shall receive the gift of the Holy Ghost" (Acts 2:38).

The true biblical Gospel always included repentance toward God.

> "I say unto you, that likewise joy shall be in heaven over **one sinner** that **repenteth,** more than over ninety and nine just persons, which need no repentance" (Luke 15:7)

The good news of the gospel is not only that Christ died and rose again the third day to save us from our sins. The good news is that our creator, a thrice holy God would love sinful man enough to desire a relationship with him, and that he wants so much to bridge the separation caused by our sin that he was willing to sacrifice his only Son to reconcile us to himself.

While we tend to focus on *coming to Christ,* in the preaching of the gospel, worshipping him *as God* (and rightfully so); the gospel message itself is not limited to Christ. It is God's plan for the salvation and reconciliation of man. It is the *gospel of God* as well as the *gospel of Christ*. The Bible even refers to the gospel as the *gospel of God* seven times in the New Testament.

> "So being affectionately desirous of you, we were willing to have imparted unto you, not the **gospel of God** only, but also our own souls, because ye were dear unto us. For ye remember, brethren, our labour and travail: for labouring night and day, because we would not be chargeable unto any of you, we preached unto you the **gospel of God**. Ye are witnesses, and God also, how holily and justly and unblameably we behaved ourselves among you that believe: As ye know how we exhorted and comforted and charged every one of you, as a father doth his children, **That ye would walk worthy of God, who hath called you unto his kingdom and glory."** (1 Thessalonians 2:8-12)

"Paul, a servant of Jesus Christ, called to be an apostle, separated unto the **gospel of God**," (Romans 1:1)

What is the message that we should be proclaiming?

Be ye reconciled to God!

> "And all things are of God, who hath reconciled us to himself by Jesus Christ, and hath given to us the ministry of reconciliation;" (2 Corinthians 5:18)

God has given to us the ministry of reconciliation. We are called to go to the world with the message of God's love for man and his plan to reconcile them to himself through Jesus Christ. Nowhere is this message of a Father's love more beautifully illustrated than in the parable of the prodigal son. This parable perfectly pictures God's desire to reconcile sinful man to himself.

The Prodigal Son

Although many teach that this parable is speaking of the backsliding believer, the context makes it clear that Jesus is referring to the salvation of a lost sinner. (The New Testament does not refer to believers as lost *or* as sinners.)

From verse one, he is speaking of the joy and value of every sinner that is saved, against the accusation of the Pharisees who condemned him for eating with such sinners. It's clear that the older brother who resented the Father's celebration upon the return of his lost son, is a picture of the Pharisees' lack of understanding of God's love and desire for the salvation of every sinner that comes to repentance and faith. This is a story that every parent should be able to relate to.

> "And he said, A certain man had two sons: And the younger of them said to his father, Father, give me the portion of goods that falleth to me. And he divided unto them his living. And not many days after the younger son gathered all together, and took his journey into a far country, and there wasted his substance with riotous living. And when he had spent all, there arose a mighty famine in that land; and he began to be in want. And he went and joined himself to a citizen of that country; and he sent him into his fields to feed swine. And he would fain have filled his belly with the husks that the swine did eat: and no man gave unto him. And when he came to himself, he said, How many hired servants of my father's have bread enough and to spare, and I perish with hunger! I will arise and go to my father, and will say unto him, Father, I have sinned against heaven, and before thee, And am no more worthy to be called thy son: make me as one of thy hired servants. And he arose, and came

to his father. But when he was yet a great way off, his father saw him, and had compassion, and ran, and fell on his neck, and kissed him. (Luke 15:11-20)

The prodigal son saw the worthlessness and destruction of his sin and sorrowed in despair. He remembered the goodness of his father and was led to repentance before him. Returning to him who gave him all good things that he ever knew, he submitted himself in contrition and humility.

"And the son said unto him, Father, I have sinned against heaven, and in thy sight, and am no more worthy to be called thy son." (Luke 15:21)

Is this not the picture of fallen man, once created in God's image, but now separated from him by sin? The son seeing his unworthiness to be recognized as a son, returned to his father humbling himself, willing even to submit unto him as a servant.

The Father would not allow his son to work for his forgiveness, but instead offered mercy and grace. He welcomed him with open arms and restored him, not as a servant, but as a son, even lavishing blessings upon him.

"But the father said to his servants, Bring forth the best robe, and put it on him; and put a ring on his hand, and shoes on his feet: And bring hither the fatted calf, and kill it; and let us eat, and be merry:" (Luke 15:22-23)

This father, so loved his son, that being reconciled to him whom he had lost to sin, was as receiving one alive that was dead.

"For this **my son was dead, and is alive again; he was lost, and is found**. And they began to be merry." (Luke 15:24)

We see that the son was *dead* and *lost*, but now is found and alive once more. It was a joyous celebration! It is the same for every sinner that comes to salvation in Christ. Through God's love, we are given what we do not deserve. We who were *lost* are found. We who were *dead* are made alive again and given the power to be called the sons of God.

The prodigal could have chosen to remain alienated in his sin and never known the blessings his Father had for him. Or he could have clung to his works insisting on earning forgiveness as a servant forever, pridefully rejecting the Father's mercy and grace. If he had not turned from his sinful life, back to the Father in repentance, none of these blessings would have been received.

Many parents have experienced the pain of having a prodigal child. After years of nourishing, teaching and giving every good thing possible, to see the child that they've loved so much grow up, and run toward sin and destruction is heartbreaking enough; but the rebellion and rejection of your love is devastating. How many sleepless nights of worry and regret have been spent by parents just wishing their child would come home?

If they did come back, even with a huge debt to pay for the choices they made, wouldn't you, like the Father, give them everything you had to save them? Of course, but wouldn't you also expect them to have a repentant attitude, as the prodigal son did? Certainly, you would.

Why is it so hard to imagine that God expects the same? Why do we refuse to believe that God desires sinners to repent? For a lost sinner to be reconciled to God, they must turn to him in order to receive the blessings he has for them. This turning is certainly not an eradication of sin, or even reformation. The prodigal by his efforts to return to his Father did not clean himself or fill his own belly or even restore his own standing as a son; but taking that step of turning from the world of sin and drawing nigh instead to his father put him in the position for the father to do all of that.

God, as our heavenly Father has gone through exactly that with us. He has experienced our rebellion and blasphemy, our disobedience and shaming of his name. Yet, when we turn to him in repentance, he gives us everything he has, even his own Son, and restores us as sons of God, lavishing upon us the manifold blessings of salvation. This is the picture of salvation for every sinner.

> "For God so loved the world, that he gave his only begotten Son, that whosoever believeth in him should not perish, but have everlasting life." (John 3:16)

We have been commissioned with the message of reconciliation to the God of the universe, who is so perfect and holy and of purer eyes than to behold iniquity. His power and his wrath are so great that none can stand against him; yet his love and mercy toward us outweighs even that. Is this the God we are presenting to the lost?

We have been sent to call sinners to be reconciled to God, leaving the paths of sin and turning to him, who as a good Father, loves them beyond measure. There is no salvation without repentance.

Recently, when witnessing to a young woman at her door, I had the opportunity to apply this principle to the gospel message I was sharing with her. She explained that she believed there was a God and tried to read her Bible; but she did not understand what it was all about. While we were talking, her son of maybe four or five years old peaked out the window. I asked her if that was her son. She beamed with joy and nodded.

I was able to then share with her the picture of God as her loving Father. I asked how she would feel if her son continually rebelled against her, disobeyed and ultimately lived as though she did not exist. She expressed the anger and crushing disappointment that she would feel. She was able to see that it probably grieved God's heart that she herself behaved that way toward him.

Presenting God as the loving parent who desires to be reconciled to her opened her heart to see his goodness. God's desire to bring her back into a right relationship made sense to her because of the love she felt for her own son.

After explaining the plan of salvation, and the tremendous sacrifice God had made for her, I asked her how she would feel toward someone who went so far to have a relationship with her.

"Would you continue to run from him and disobey him? Would you live as though he did not exist, as you did before?" I asked.

"Oh no." she said. "I would be grateful."

Through this, she was able to see not only her sin and disobedience toward God, but also his love, as well as his righteous judgment of her sin and rejection of him.

As we talked, some of her friends came out on the porch and took the conversation a different direction, but I believe that her heart was broken for the Lord and that a seed was planted that evening. (We will look at more sample conversations and ideas for evangelism in chapter 10).

When we are sharing the gospel message with the lost it's important to look for evidences of good soil. Is there a desire to be right with God, or indifference? Are they still, as the prodigal son chasing after their lusts while running from the Father's presence, or have they come to the place where they want to return to God? If not, the gospel is only foolishness to them. Their sin has yet blinded them to their need for a Savior.

I hear so many soul winners talk about those who have heard and seem to understand the gospel, but just will not give in and accept salvation. Honestly, how hard is it to see that they will not accept it because they do not yet believe they need it? If they truly believed that they were condemned sinners before a holy God, who could at any moment send them to an eternity in hell, we would not have to persuade them to accept salvation.

The problem is that either they do not believe they

deserve it, or that God will really do it. They do not really believe God. They will not acknowledge him or glorify him as God. They minimize his righteousness and holiness as well as his right to punish sin, thus justifying their own standing before him. They must believe the reality of their condemnation before they can desire salvation.

Often, these who will not obey God are told to simply decide to accept Jesus. We do not receive Christ by our prayer or by our will, but by faith. Notice here in John 1:12-13 that they that received Christ by faith, were not born again of the will, but of God.

> "But as many as received him, to them gave he power to become the sons of God, even to them that believe on his name: Which were born, not of blood, **nor of the will of the flesh, nor of the will of man,** but of God." (John 1:12-13)

A lost man who genuinely comes to a knowledge of the precious gift of salvation by the sacrifice of Christ should not need to be pressed for a decision or fed the words of a prayer in order to profess his belief. Coming to a knowledge of the truth of what Christ has done for a hopeless, condemned sinner should not produce indifference or indecision.

Instead, you should expect him to heartily embrace the truth of the gospel joyously crying (at least in his heart), "Eureka! I have found it! I was lost, but now am found, was blind but now I see!" Genuine salvation will always show in our verbal conversation as well as in the fruits will be in our lives.

In the Scriptures, salvation is pictured as going from darkness to light, the opening of blind eyes, or the dead raised to new life. Could a spiritually dead man be brought to new life or a blind man receive his sight and not want to profess his belief in this great and precious Savior?

When this is not the reaction we see, many soul winners

press those who do not yet understand or embrace the precious truth of the gospel, who's eyes have not yet been opened, to simply call upon the Lord through prayer, implying that it is their prayer or decision saves them.

If we push someone for a decision to accept Christ when they have not yet truly believed, what we are really doing is encouraging them to draw nigh with their mouth and honor him with their lips; while their hearts are far from him. How can we possibly believe this lip-service is pleasing to God?

We are saved by God's grace through the instrument of faith, not through a prayer. God chose the foolishness of preaching (the gospel) to save them that believe. (1Corinthians 1:21) Why? Because "…faith cometh by hearing…" (Romans 10:17)

If we must press for a decision, shouldn't that be to turn to God in repentance and agree with him about their sin? If they have not seen their need for a Savior, then clearly, they do not yet comprehend their condemnation before God. They may even need more awareness of sin, or conviction by the Holy Spirit to bring them to repentance so that the word of faith can take root in their hearts.

Evidences of conviction

Since we know that a heart that is still hardened with sin cannot allow the seed of the gospel to penetrate, it is important that we look for evidences of conviction and repentance. Are they convinced of sin, or still arguing and excusing it? Many people will readily admit that they have sinned, but do not have a sense of the seriousness of that sin.

They might say things like, *"Yes, I've lied; but everybody has."* Or, *"Yes, I stole years ago, but I don't do that anymore."* Qualifiers such as these attached to their admissions indicate a lack of genuine acknowledgement of their sinfulness. They are not owning the sinfulness within that causes them to sin. They are still justifying themselves by comparison to others or to their present circumstances.

Keep in mind that the god of this world has blinded (hardened) them which believe not lest the glorious light of the gospel shine unto them. At this point, it is still only foolishness to them.

How does Satan blind them? The same way he did with Eve. Through the deceitfulness of sin, tempting her to disobey God. Eve was tempted by the lust of her eyes and the pride of life. She saw that the forbidden fruit was good for food and able to make one as God. She wanted to taste it as well as benefit from the power promised within it. Eve wanted to be *as* God.

It is the same for all of us. We are all tempted when we are drawn away by our lust. Whether it be the lust of the flesh, the lust of the eyes, or the pride of life makes, no difference; because "...when lust hath conceived, it bringeth forth sin: and sin, when it is finished, bringeth forth death." (James 1:15)

Until they become guilty before God, they will not believe that they are condemned by God and in need of a Savior. Compared to everyone else, they may think they aren't so bad, because they do not yet understand that God expects perfect righteousness. Jesus said that "... except your righteousness shall exceed the righteousness of the scribes and Pharisees, ye shall in no case enter into the kingdom of heaven." (Matthew 5:20)

Even Paul, a Pharisee, had to come to a knowledge of his own sin in order to understand the need for a Savior. What was it that showed Paul his sin?

By the law is the knowledge of sin.

> "Now we know that what things soever the law saith, it saith to them who are under the law: that every mouth may be stopped, and all the world may become guilty befoe God." (Romans 3:19)

By the law comes not only the knowledge of sin, but the knowledge of God's righteousness and his just judgment of their sin.

> "Wherefore the law is holy, and the commandment holy, and just, and good. Was then that which is good made death unto me? God forbid. But sin, that it might appear sin, working death in me by that which is good; that sin by the commandment might become exceeding sinful." (Romans 7:12-13)

Through the law, man is brought to see sin the way God sees it. Sin becomes exceedingly sinful, while God's righteous standard is holy and just and good. They see their just condemnation before God and the arguments cease. The law stops their mouth.

If they continue to reject the law of God, then they must be warned of the destruction of sin. They must understand that they have *already* been condemned by their sin and that God *will* punish them.

Although God is love, he is also still the same God he has always been. The God who struck Nadab and Abihu for offering strange fire is the same God who struck Uzza dead for reaching his hand out to steady the ark. This same God is the God who will judge their sin because he is "...holy and of purer eyes than to behold evil, and canst not look on iniquity:" (Habakkuk 1:13)

> "It is a fearful thing to fall into the hands of the living God." (Hebrews 10:31)

Those who receive the word gladly

For those who are under conviction and do desire to be reconciled to God, the gospel of Jesus Christ truly is good news. The lost soul who sees his sin and condemnation before God receives the gospel as light shining through the darkness opening his blind eyes.

So, how then do we counsel those who hear the word and receive it gladly? Many would suggest leading them through a prayer to quickly seal the deal before they change their minds. This does not seem to be the answer Jesus would have given though.

I know that this goes against the grain of the Easy Believism gospel most have been taught; but if we are to evangelize after Jesus' pattern, we must counsel those who claim to desire salvation to count the cost.

We would never want to discourage anyone from receiving Christ, but clearly, Christ did counsel those who desired to follow him to consider the consequences of their decision. He did not beg them to follow him, but told them that if they would, they must *deny themselves and take up their cross.*

> "And whosoever doth not **bear his cross**, and come after me, cannot be my disciple. For which of you, intending to build a tower, sitteth not down first, and counteth the cost, whether he have sufficient to finish it? Lest haply, after he hath laid the foundation, and is not able to finish it, all that behold it begin to mock him, Saying, This man began to build, and was not able to finish." (Luke 14:27-30)

Jesus called his disciples to leave family, friends, and the cares of the world behind to follow him.

> "And another also said, Lord, I will follow thee; but let me first go bid them farewell, which are at home at my house. And Jesus said unto him, **No man, having put his hand to the plough, and looking back, is fit for the kingdom of God**. (Luke 9:61)

> "… **If any man will come after me, let him deny himself, and take up his cross, and follow me.**"

(Matthew 16:24)

"But Jesus said unto him, **Follow me; and let the dead bury their dead.**" (Matthew 8:22)

This may seem like a counterproductive way to make disciples, but if the lost man is not willing to take up his cross, then he obviously does not see its worth.

Keep in mind that our holy and righteous God showed his great love to us by offering the greatest sacrifice ever given. We should not be twisting the arms of sinners to accept Christ. We should be calling them to humble themselves before God and repent of their sin in gratitude for the salvation he has provided in Jesus Christ. Those who see and embrace this precious gift of salvation should have the desire to follow Christ *at any cost*.

Should we pray with them?

I would never discourage prayer; but remember that it is *not* the prayer or confession that saves, but genuine faith. The confession of faith should be something they express without coercion, because it is the outflowing of what is in their heart already.

If we lead people to believe that a prayer is what secures salvation and then lead them to pray, naturally they will believe that they have fulfilled the requirements and are indeed saved. But as we well know, not every prayer is from the heart of faith. Reciting a prayer for a Catholic or other works-based background can easily become just another work on their checklist instead of their heart's cry of faith in the Savior. That's why it is very important that we do not suggest something to *do* to secure salvation. Using biblical terminology helps to avoid such issues.

If someone asks me to pray with them, often I will pray aloud asking God to help them to repent of their sins and come to saving faith. If they have already expressed their belief to me, I will ask God to give them assurance through the indwelling Holy Spirit and help them to testify of their new faith through believer's baptism.

Christ called us, *not* to collect decisions, but to baptize believers and make disciples.

"Go ye therefore, and teach all nations, baptizing them in the name of the Father, and of the Son, and of the Holy Ghost: Teaching them to observe all things whatsoever I have commanded you: and, lo, I am with you alway, even unto the end of the world. Amen." (Matthew 28:19)

Often, I hear testimonies about those who were led through a prayer and pronounced saved, but none ever show up at church or claim that salvation themselves through being baptized. We should always instruct new believers to be baptized.

If we only lead people through prayers, we have not fulfilled the Great Commission. Many will profess belief in Christ, but remember, even the demons believe and tremble. Obedience to Christ is the truest evidence of genuine belief.

Submitting to the ordinance of baptism is the very first test of obedience for the believer. This is also often the first public testimony of association with Christ as his follower. A believer who will not publicly profess his faith through baptism, who is ashamed of Christ has a shaky testimony of faith.

The second test for the new Christian is to join themselves to the church in order to be taught as a disciple and member of the body.

"Then they that gladly received his word were baptized: and the same day there were added unto them about three thousand souls. **And they continued stedfastly in the apostles' doctrine and fellowship,**

and in breaking of bread, and in prayers." (Acts 2:41)

If we were to count our converts by these evidences alone, rather than by sinner's prayers, our numbers would be significantly lower than what we currently claim.

If we only lead them through a prayer and then leave them in the same state that we found them, as servants of sin, who are unwilling to follow Christ, the evidence would suggest that we have not really *led them to the Lord*.

CHAPTER 8
GIVING ASSURANCE OF SALVATION

Many soul-winning courses teach that we should immediately offer assurance of salvation to those who profess belief. I believe this practice was originally intended to give believers knowledge of their eternal security, *if* they are indeed saved.

Teaching the eternal security of the genuine believer is a biblical doctrine and a very necessary truth. A born-again believer certainly needs to understand that they cannot lose their salvation. *If* they are saved, they are secure.

Assuring a *professing* believer, however, that they *are* genuinely saved is a very different issue. This is something we cannot possibly know for them. Only they themselves and the Lord can know this with any certainty. We cannot know their hearts or the truth of their regeneration. We can only view the outward evidences, or lack thereof.

As we have already seen, a profession, baptism, or even initial excitement expressed by the professing believer is not proof. Often these things are not genuine.

Assuring someone else of salvation is, in my opinion, quite possibly *the most dangerous aspect* of today's modern gospel. We cannot assure anyone of that which we cannot know. If we do nothing else, I pray that we will at the very least, *stop* assuring others of their salvation!

I recently heard the testimonies of two separate individuals who shared a lack of assurance in their salvations. The first stated that she did not know how or when she had gotten saved, but that some women had given her a Bible and written her name in it, telling her that she was.

The other was a gentleman who stated that he wasn't sure when he was saved either, because he had gotten saved a bunch of times. He testified of living in blatant, unrepentant sin for most of his professed Christian life. Although he could not identify a specific time when he had come to repentance and the knowledge of salvation through faith or even recall a time when he was certain that he had been born again; he had prayed the sinner's prayer many times.

Both of their testimonies showed an obvious lack of understanding regarding the nature of salvation that needed to be addressed before even possibly offering assurances. Salvation demands a knowledge of the truth.

Some Christian denominations teach that you can be saved and then lose your salvation. Because of this, many professing Christians, like the man mentioned above, believe that they must get saved over and over, or reaffirm their commitment to Christ many times throughout their lives in order to keep themselves saved. They pray the Sinner's Prayer each time, expecting to be renewed unto repentance and claiming Christ's blood once again. Hebrews chapter six proves that this is not possible.

> "For it is impossible for those who were once enlightened, and have tasted of the heavenly gift, and were made partakers of the Holy Ghost, And have tasted the good word of God, and the powers of the world to come, If they shall fall away, to renew them again unto repentance; seeing they crucify to themselves the Son of God afresh, and put him to an open shame." (Hebrews 6:4-6)

To be saved over and over is simply not possible. Professing believers such as this were more than likely never genuinely saved at all; because they do not yet understand.

> "Who will have all men to be saved, and to come unto the knowledge of the truth." (1 Timothy 2:4)

Many Christians, instead of offering counsel to address such issues, immediately offer assurance of salvation, assuring the professing believer that *whosoever calleth upon the name of Lord shall be saved*, and that if they called (prayed a prayer), then they are saved and just doubting. How sad that so many put more stock in a prayer than in coming to genuine faith through a knowledge of the truth.

Our words of confession are one of the ways we show our faith. It is evidence to others, as well as to us that our faith is genuine. When the Holy Spirit of God within a believing heart prompts someone (without the coercion of others) to testify of Christ and willingly associate their lives with him, it can be a very assuring evidence to that believer.

If that confession, however, is merely a reluctant agreement to pray because of the promise of heaven, it may convince the soul winner; but often the professing convert is left unconvinced, because the assurance came from *without* rather than from *within*.

> "Hereby know we that we dwell in him, and he in us, because he hath given us of his Spirit." (1 John 4:13)

Notice, that according to the Bible, it is by the presence of the Holy Spirit that a believer knows they are saved. We cannot know that for them. We can only observe the evidences of such, or lack thereof.

If we are going to give assurance, shouldn't we ourselves at least be convinced by a preponderance of evidence? Helping them to settle the matter of their salvation is for them, everlasting *life or death!* Who are we to offer assurance of that which we cannot possibly be certain?

Are we convinced by a preponderance of evidence?

Or could it be that we are simply leaning to our own understanding according to the methods and message we have been taught?

It honestly makes me wonder why we are so anxious to offer assurances to others, when we can never know. What if the Holy Spirit is convicting them of their lost condition? We could easily be counseling them in a way that quenches the Spirit. If they are merely professing without possessing, while living in rebellion to God, we could be helping them to harden their hearts against God.

Even if we sincerely believed that they showed evidence of salvation at one time, but now were in sin, why would we not warn them to turn from their sin? Either way, they are in spiritual danger and repentance is called for. It would seem to me that, if they are living in sin, we should warn them and do what the Bible says is best, not comfort them and lull them back to their spiritual sleep.

What would make us so committed to defending the authenticity of their salvation without any legitimate evidence? When we look at it considering their possible destruction, it almost seems as though we are more concerned with defending our beliefs than we are about their souls.

I wonder, if we were forced to see that these converts were not saved, would we also have to admit that our own converts were probably not saved as well? I understand full well the difficulty of accepting such truth.

Years ago, when I began to see that most of my own converts did not evidence salvation in any way, it was difficult to accept that I had possibly led them into a false assurance. Not only was it humbling personally to admit that I had led them to believe something that was not true; it was horrifying to think of the consequences of such error! These souls that I had so longed to see saved, were quite possibly further from the truth for having heard my own message of *just say this prayer*.

Those who have spent years practicing this type of

evangelism have, not only a loyalty to the message they have preached, but an emotional investment as well. Many have a list of names in the backs of their Bibles, along with a list of close relatives that they have claimed as converts. Accepting the fact that our own children may be among them makes it even more heart wrenching. We all have children who we thought were saved and now pray will one day return to church.

We must ask ourselves, will we continue to lean to our own understanding and assure converts, as well as our own adult children of our *just say this prayer* gospel? Or will we seek to genuinely assist them in finding the truth of their eternal destination?

Often, when attempting to give assurance, the questions asked are based upon our own faulty evangelism method and not reliable in determining true salvation. These questions generally sound something like this:

"Did you ask Jesus into your heart?"
"Did you call upon the name of the Lord, or pray a prayer?"
"Did you believe in the death burial and resurrection of Christ?"
(Remember, even the demons believe and tremble).

These questions are not reliable determinations of salvation. These only assess their compliance with our method of salvation. We need to look for biblical evidences. Does the biblical evidence point to spiritual life or to death?

"For **a good tree bringeth not forth corrupt fruit**; neither doth a corrupt tree bring forth good fruit. For every tree is known by his own fruit. For of thorns men do not gather figs, nor of a bramble bush gather they grapes. **A good man out of the good treasure of his heart bringeth forth that which is good; and an evil man out of the evil treasure of his heart bringeth forth that which is evil**: for of the abundance of the heart his mouth speaketh. (Luke 6:43-45)

Examining the evidences of someone else's salvation is not to judge or condemn, but to assist them in finding the truth. Again, we can never be sure of anyone else's salvation; but if we genuinely desire to help them find the truth, we must look for biblical evidences.

What Salvation Looks Like

If we are going to give someone assurance of salvation based upon the visible evidences; then obviously, we need to have an idea of what salvation *looks like* in order to contrast it with what the unsaved man looks like.

In the book of Galatians, we find these contrasted already for us. The unsaved man is presented first according to the works of the flesh that he often displays. Then, we see the saved man manifesting the fruit of the Spirit.

> "Now the works of the flesh are manifest, which are these; Adultery, fornication, uncleanness, lasciviousness, Idolatry, witchcraft, hatred, variance, emulations, wrath, strife, seditions, heresies, Envyings, murders, drunkenness, revellings, and such like: of the which I tell you before, as I have also told you in time past, that **they which do such things shall not inherit the kingdom of God**." (Galatians 5:19-21)

> "But the fruit of the Spirit is love, joy, peace, longsuffering, gentleness, goodness, faith, Meekness, temperance: against such there is no law." (Galatians 5:22-23)

In Romans, we have another picture of the lost man.

> "Being filled with all unrighteousness, fornication, wickedness, covetousness, maliciousness; full of envy,

murder, debate, deceit, malignity; whisperers, Backbiters, haters of God, despiteful, proud, boasters, inventors of evil things, disobedient to parents, Without understanding, covenantbreakers, without natural affection, implacable, unmerciful: Who knowing the judgment of God, that they which commit such things are worthy of death, not only do the same, but have pleasure in them that do them." (Romans 1:29-32)

In 1Corinthians chapter 6, we see another contrast of the lost man with the *now saved*, who evidenced the same works of the flesh at one time, but who are now, washed, justified and sanctified.

"Know ye not that the unrighteous shall not inherit the kingdom of God? **Be not deceived**: neither fornicators, nor idolaters, nor adulterers, nor effeminate, nor abusers of themselves with mankind, Nor thieves, nor covetous, nor drunkards, nor revilers, nor extortioners, **shall inherit the kingdom of God.** And such **were** some of you: but ye **are** washed, but ye are sanctified, but ye are justified in the name of the Lord Jesus, and by the Spirit of our God." (1 Corinthians 6:9)

"For this ye know, that no whoremonger, nor unclean person, nor covetous man, who is an idolater, hath any inheritance in the kingdom of Christ and of God. **Let no man deceive you** with vain words: **for** because of these things cometh the wrath of God upon the children of disobedience." (Ephesians 5:5-6)

If we see these things in the life of a professing believer, how could we *not* warn them of their possible destruction? While these are very visible ways that we can observe works of the flesh or fruit of the Spirit, not every lost man displays such visible evidences. There are many moral people who are unsaved. Therefore, it is not always easy for us to even form an opinion based on these alone. We also need to ask questions, get to know them and help them to see whether their testimony points to salvation.

The *only genuine assurance* of salvation comes from within the believer by *the presence of the indwelling Holy Spirit*. Attempting to assess the evidences of such is the basis of our next examination.

Let me sy without apology that there is no way for the Holy Spirit of our living God to enter a spiritually dead sinner and *not* make himself known. Being regenerated is a radically transforming event. The Holy Spirit *will* make his presence known. That is a Bible fact.

> "The Spirit itself beareth witness with our spirit, that we are the children of God:" (Romans 8:16)

"And hereby we know that he abideth in us, by the Spirit which he hath given us" (1 John 3:24).

The question we should be asking them is if they have been born-again. Have they received the in-dwelling Holy Spirit since they have claimed to be saved? When the apostle Paul passed through the upper coasts of Ephesus, he found certain disciples and "He said unto them, Have ye received the Holy Ghost since ye believed?" (Acts 19:2)

Is this not a valid question for believers today? Have you received the Holy Ghost? This, of course is not to demand evidence of the Holy Spirit through signs and wonders, but by the evidences listed in the book of 1 John whereby a born-again believer can know that he is truly in Christ.

Have you been born-again since you claimed to have believed? Have you been regenerated, brought to new life, and become the new creature that God describes a true believer to be?

More questions to aid in assessing the presence of the Holy Spirit within the professing believer:

Do they have a clear understanding of the gospel message? Many people hear the gospel message but do not completely understand all that it means. Many false religions, such as Catholicism have adopted our terminology and will say the same things that we say, while meaning something very different.

For instance: A Catholic may say that they are saved (born-again even) by grace, through faith in Christ. This of course makes it sound as though they agree with the biblical message of salvation. But according to Catholic teaching, what that really means is that they are saved by the grace that is conferred to them through sacraments of the Catholic Church *and* faith in Jesus Christ. Sacraments plus faith in Christ is a works-based salvation, not the salvation by grace through faith that we teach.

As a former Catholic, I can testify that as a child, I believed in God. I even believed that Jesus Christ was the sinless Son of God who died, was buried and rose again to pay for my sins. I was not however saved, because I also believed that my own works of righteousness (sacraments) were helping to save me as well. I was still blind to the truth of the gospel and trusting in a false religion.

> "In whom the god of this world hath blinded the minds of them which believe not, lest the light of the glorious gospel of Christ, who is the image of God, should shine unto them." (2 Corinthians 4:4)

Unless we dig a little and ask questions, we cannot know how they are understanding salvation, or if they are still blinded.

Does their testimony include repentance? Today, it is quite common to hear testimonies of those who have accepted Christ, according to an Easy Believism gospel without repentance toward God.

As we have already seen, there is no salvation without

repentance. Christ came to call sinners to repentance, not the righteous. If they have not come to an awareness of their sin and condemnation, how can they believe on Christ as their Savior?

> "The Lord is not slack concerning his promise, as some men count slackness; but is longsuffering to us-ward, not willing that any should perish, but that all should come to repentance." (2 Peter 3:9)

Does their life show evidence of reconciliation to God? Was there any point at which there was a visible indication of having turned to God for reconciliation? Or do they appear to have continued in enmity against God?

Often, I hear Christians suggest that people are just backslidden; but in order to slide backward, don't they have to be going in the right direction initially? For many converts, this is not the case. They have prayed a prayer but have never repented or turned toward God at all. They are not backslidden, but continuing in the direction of sin that they have always been in.

Some are stony ground hearers at best, receiving the message happily, but having no root within themselves, never producing the genuine fruit of saving faith.

Was their profession a public testimony of association with Christ as his follower? Did they join themselves to the church and show their faith through believer's baptism and continue in fellowship and doctrine? Or was their profession only a coerced prayer to save them from Hell?

> "Then they that gladly received his word were baptized: and the same day there were added unto them about three thousand souls. And they continued stedfastly in the apostles' doctrine and fellowship, and in breaking of bread, and in prayers." (Acts 2:41-42)

Is there a testimony of new life? Can they say without compulsion, that they have been born-again? *I once was lost but now am found?* Did salvation make them a new creature with a new world view, and perspective on sin?

"Therefore if any man be in Christ, he is a new creature: old things are passed away; behold, all things are become new." (2 Corinthians 5:17)

Did their salvation give them a love for the brethren? Do they embrace other believers as their community or are they still more comfortable with those of the world? The Holy Spirit gives us a love for the brethren. Those who were once peculiar laughingstocks become those that we desire to spend time with and be like.

"We know that we have passed from death unto life, because we love the brethren. He that loveth not his brother abideth in death." (1 John 3:14)

Has their salvation given them a desire to please God? The Holy Spirit within the believer desires to please God, and so leads the believer in the same desires. This can be very difficult (if not impossible) for us to discern, but we can certainly ask questions.

Do they appear to walk as closely as they can with the Lord, or see how far they can push the limits, only going through the motions of religion? Do they argue against the sinfulness of sin or has the righteousness of the law shut their mouths? Even sincere believers will fall at times, but the Holy Spirit within them assures that they cannot comfortably excuse it away and dwell in that sin for long.

"And hereby we do know that we know him, if we keep his commandments. He that saith, I know him, and keepeth not his commandments, is a liar, and the truth is not in him. But whoso keepeth his word, in him verily is the love of God perfected: hereby know we that we are in him." (1 John 2:3-5)

Has their salvation given them a love for the word? Do they search the Scriptures daily to learn more of God or is their daily Bible reading a chore? The Holy Spirit gives us a love for his word, and a desire to know him through it.

"As newborn babes, desire the sincere milk of the word, that ye may grow thereby:" (1 Peter 2:2)

Do they evidence fruit of the Spirit; or are the works of the flesh more evident in their lives?

"Now the works of the flesh are manifest, which are these; Adultery, fornication, uncleanness, lasciviousness, Idolatry, witchcraft, hatred, variance, emulations, wrath, strife, seditions, heresies, Envyings, murders, drunkenness, revellings, and such like: of the which I tell you before, as I have also told you in time past, that **they which do such things shall not inherit the kingdom of God.** But the fruit of the Spirit is love, joy, peace, longsuffering, gentleness, goodness, faith, Meekness, temperance: against such there is no law. (Galatians 5:19-23)

If the preponderance of evidence points to a lack of salvation, what reason could we possibly have to assure them falsely? Love would demand the truth. If our best guess is only a guess, shouldn't we err on the side of caution and warn them of their imminent danger?

Telling a saved person that lives like the unsaved that they may not actually be saved can do them no eternal harm. It could, in fact, lead them to repentance and restored fellowship. On the other hand, if we assure a lost person who is living in sin that they are saved; we could very well be doing them eternal harm.

If we change nothing else in our evangelism, *we must at least stop offering our own assurances to others.* The Bible says to work out *your own* salvation. It says to examine *yourself* to see if you are in the faith. The only genuine assurance anyone can ever have is that which comes from God through the indwelling Holy Spirit.

> "Hereby know we that we dwell in him, and he in us, because he hath given us of his Spirit." (1 John 4:13)

If they fear and doubt, let us offer to them biblical answers by pointing them to the Scriptures instead of our evangelism philosophies.

> "Herein is our love made perfect, that we may have boldness in the day of judgment: because as he is, so are we in this world. ..." (1 John 4:17)

If they do not have assurance, we must allow them to consider the possibility that they have not been made perfect in love. They may even have a reason to fear the day of judgment. In that case, the most loving thing we could do for them is to instruct them to repent and seek reconciliation with God as we would any lost person.

CHAPTER 9
CONTINUATION

The final *evidence* (not proof) of genuine salvation is continuation in the faith. A failure to continue in the faith, according to Scripture, is an indication that salvation was not genuine. This is something that goes against everything that modern Christianity teaches, and sadly, the following Scripture seems to be the hardest for us to accept.

> "They went out from us, but they were not of us; for if they had been of us, they would no doubt have continued with us: **but they went out, that they might be made manifest that they were not all of us.**" (1 John 2:19)

It does not get much clearer than that. Does your convert continue to walk with the Lord?

I often hear people talk about how their children got saved and were so excited for the Lord, witnessing to their friends and participating zealously in ministries at church; but then these children simply grew up and fell away. Nevertheless, they insist that their children are saved and do not even consider the possibility that they may be in danger of eternal destruction.

As we saw in the parable of the sower, those who fall away (or are offended) never produced the fruit of saving faith, much as the *Lord, Lord* converts of Matthew chapter seven. These may behave as Christians for a time and even be convinced that they *are* Christians; but they were never truly saved.

The apostle Paul was concerned with the state of his converts, continually writing to them and exhorting them to *continue* in the faith. This was not to hold on to their salvation, but to assure themselves and Paul of the genuineness of their salvation. Clearly, the lack of continuation led to a loss of assurance. It only makes sense that someone who falls away would doubt their own salvation. Continuation evidences genuine faith and helps assure them of their standing in Christ.

A walk that is marked by continual backsliding or falling away instead of continuing to perfection is an indication of unbelief not faith. A Christian's walk should not be characterized by such froward behavior but by continuation. Paul teaches them that those who are saved should bring forth fruits meet for their Savior.

> "For the earth which drinketh in the rain that cometh oft upon it, and bringeth forth herbs meet for them by whom it is dressed, receiveth blessing from God:" (Hebrews 6:7)

But he that brings forth briars and thorns is *"nigh unto cursing"* whose end is eternal fire.

> "But that which beareth thorns and briers is rejected, and is **nigh unto cursing; whose end is to be burned.**" (Heb. 6: 8)

This is the same principle Jesus set forth in Matthew.

> "Even so **every good tree bringeth forth good fruit**; but a corrupt tree bringeth forth evil fruit. A good tree cannot bring forth evil fruit, neither can a corrupt tree bring forth good fruit. Every tree **that bringeth not forth good fruit is hewn down, and cast into the fire.**" (Matthew 7:17-19)

This should be a sobering thought. Again, this is not to say that they must maintain good works to keep salvation or that anyone could *lose* their salvation, but to say that their actions testify either to their belief or their unbelief. If they are saved, their works should not be choked out by the thorns and briars of sin, falling away as unbelievers do. Genuine salvation is evidenced by good fruits and a continuation in the faith.

"Wherefore the rather, brethren, give diligence to make your calling and election sure: for if ye do these things, ye shall never fall:" (2 Peter 1:10)

"Being confident of this very thing, that he which hath begun a good work in you will perform it until the day of Jesus Christ:" (Philippians 1:6)

Part of being confident in our eternal security comes from the knowledge that we are no longer the same person we were before. We are a new creature in Christ. We have been raised in newness of life and are being conformed to the image of Christ through the process of sanctification. We have been predestinated to be conformed to the image of Christ.

"For whom he did foreknow, he also did predestinate to be conformed to the image of his Son, that he might be the firstborn among many brethren. Moreover whom he did predestinate, them he also called: and whom he called, them he also justified: and whom he justified, them he also glorified." (Romans 8:29-30)

A person who *can* continue being the same person he was prior to conversion or return to that former state and dwell there comfortably, simply has not become a new creature.

When the Holy Spirit of God comes to live within the body of a believer, bringing them to new spiritual life, it is impossible for that person *not* to change. That Holy Spirit is the Spirit of God with the mind of God and the desires of God and will witness of itself giving the believer a new heart with new desires.

When that Christian behaves in a way that is contrary to the will of God, the Spirit within him will not allow him to continue in that disobedience for long; but will convict him and cause him *dis*comfort. The Spirit itself cannot dwell comfortably in disobedience to God. A genuinely bornagain person simply will not be *able* to live the way the unsaved live.

> "Seeing then that we have a great high priest, that is passed into the heavens, Jesus the Son of God, **let us hold fast our profession.**" (Hebrews 4:14)

Chastening

> "Ye have not yet resisted unto blood, striving against sin. And ye have forgotten the exhortation which speaketh unto you as unto children, My son, despise not thou the chastening of the Lord, nor faint when thou art rebuked of him: **For whom the Lord loveth he chasteneth,** and scourgeth every son whom he receiveth. **If ye endure chastening, God dealeth with you as with sons;** for what son is he whom the father chasteneth not? **But if ye be without chastisement**, whereof all are partakers, then are **ye bastards, and not sons**." (Hebrews 12:4-8)

It would be quite difficult to miss the message here. If we are Christians, (sons) we will be chastened when we wander out of the way. If God does not chasten us; but allows us to live comfortably in sin and out of fellowship with him, that can only mean that we are not sons.

This does not mean that every sin will bring chastisement, or immediately indicates a lack of salvation.

Even a just man will fall, but his direction and his purpose will continue. He may slip off the path or make a wrong turn, but his desire will be to continue seeking the Lord.

Someone who is unsaved may try to walk the same path for a time, but because he has not become a new creature with new desires, his desires continue to be those of the unsaved and will eventually lead him back to where he came from.

Discerning continuation in children

Children can be difficult to discern, because, as kids they go to church and follow our program of worship under our authority. It can be easy to assume that an obedient child who does not fuss at church attendance is saved. Don't forget that we are also their regular source of entertainment, games, prizes, snacks, events…etc.

They may even parrot our catch phrases and claim to evangelize others, seeking our approval, but the truest test comes when they are no longer under our authority, or when they outgrow our kids' clubs. Do they continue? Or do they walk away?

If they continue, is there genuine evidence of the Holy Spirit such as love for brethren, love for the word, obedience to God? Or is it merely religion? I know we have all seen Jehovah's witnesses who are extremely zealous yet are not saved. There are also, Catholics, Mormons, and Lutherans, and other mainline denominations who are not born again, but faithfully follow man's religion for whatever reason. Pharisees who seek to establish their own righteousness, going through the motions to appear godly while their hearts are far from God, can seem very committed, but eventually, works of the flesh, (as we looked at in Galatians) manifest themselves exposing their unregenerate hearts.

It can be very easy to convince ourselves that our children are saved when we see them follow our example for so many years. We may not even be alarmed when the begin to dabble in sin, assuring ourselves that they are yet saved. When they come to the place however that they have completely abandoned church and are living comfortably apart from God, we sure better be alarmed!

That is why we need to continue their training as long as we possibly can, even until adulthood, not resting our hopes on a childhood prayer.

CHAPTER 10
PUTTING IT INTO PRACTICE

If I were reading this book, the question I would have at this point is, "now that I understand the importance of repentance and of a biblical gospel message, how do I put it into practice?"

In this chapter, I'd like to present some opportunities for evangelism, conversation starters, how to avoid rabbit trails, and basic do's and don'ts for evangelism. I'd also like to offer some valuable resources that may aid in your efforts.

This is not a crash course on *getting people saved*. It is an introduction to sharing the complete gospel message (including repentance from sin) to the lost world. There are no short cuts and no foolproof ways to make converts, only false converts.

If the Lord calls you to sow or water, instead of seeing a harvest of souls, be thankful to be used in this precious work, and know that he is pleased with your faithful service.

Our goal should be to lead them to repentance toward God *and* faith in Christ, through the preaching of the word. If we preach the true gospel, we have done what is commanded.

Opportunities for evangelism

Tracts- The easiest way to share the gospel is simply by handing one to someone on the street, including one with your monthly bill, or leaving them where the unsaved will find them. This is simple, non-confrontational evangelism.

Passing out tracts at parades- The more seed you sow the more chance of bringing forth fruit unto the Lord. The easiest way to broadcast the word to large numbers of people is at parades. You can distribute hundreds of tracts in a very short amount of time. All you need are a couple of people to walk each side of the street and hand each one a tract. You might say something like, "did you get one of these?" or "can I hand you a tract?" (or brochure if that's more comfortable for you). Or you can put them in a clear bag, with a small gift or candy. You would be surprised at how many people are excited and happy to accept anything you give them. Very few people refuse, and those that do, are generally not anxious to make a scene in front of such a large crowd of onlookers.

It's best to get there ahead of the parade, as soon as people are assembling. That way you are not walking in front of people or distracting them from the view of the parade.

Fairs & festivals- Passing out tracts at festivals is also a quick and easy way to distribute a lot quickly. You can also register to set up a booth. We have done this type of evangelism many times with great success! We usually use a tabletop 3-door board display with a question on the outside of each door and the answer inside. Others use a simple illustration or poster to attract attention.

People enjoy coming up to the booth to *Take the good person test*. This is based upon the Ten Commandments, testing a person's *goodness* according to God's standard. We have also used the theme of *See three things God can't do. (Lie, Change, or let anyone into heaven unless they are born again)*. These are a great way to initiate spiritual conversations and share the gospel.

You can offer a trivial prize for taking the test. We always make sure to have free Bibles, booklets and other literature available as well. People seem quite comfortable walking up to the booth and engaging in conversation. I believe this neutral territory is perhaps less threatening to them than approaching them at their home.

Street evangelism/Preach-O-Matic- I recently met a great group of people whose ministry is to college campuses. They go onto the campus and set up a portable display, do open air preaching, and distribute literature to students. I love this and hope to partner with them again soon!

This *is* the next generation. Many young people in college today have either been disillusioned with modern Christianity or educated right out of belief in God; but many are still teachable and can be influenced. There are several different ministries that organize this type of outreach. Find one online and be a part of this much needed work.

The Preach-O-Matic is a portable display board with a built-in storage cabinet that is mounted on a two-wheeled dolly, making it super easy to set up and tear down quickly and easily. You can find them on-line or build your own.

Train stations bus stations- Like fairs and festivals, often people are comfortable speaking with you in a neutral environment rather than at their door. Offer a tract and attempt to initiate conversation. Some people may have time to kill and appreciate the company.

Door to door- Even if they aren't home, or don't answer, leaving a tract gets the gospel into that home. That tract you leave may be the only gospel they ever hear.

Conversation starters

The biggest fear in evangelizing is not knowing what to say. I'm sure it goes without saying that the most important thing is not what you say but being prayerful and being led by the Spirit; but at the same time, you need to be able to engage the lost in meaningful conversation.

The Way of the Master training program by Ray Comfort, was hugely beneficial in my soul winning efforts. I'm not completely familiar with his views on other things, so I would suggest further research. I do not follow him for other teachings but his *Hell's Best Kept Secret*, and the *Way of the Master* training, however, helped me learn how to initiate conversation, organizing key thoughts, and by providing a practical application of the law. This training program is great for group study, or individual. I have gone through this course with several groups. It's a great way to get people prepared and excited to go and witness. It even challenges the participants to go on a planned outing to apply the principles they've learned.

The *Do you consider yourself to be a good person?* approach they teach is a great place to start. It will help build confidence as you learn to share the gospel more freely.

I don't recommend using any program or method *word for word*. No rote presentation can address every issue; but if you can find something, like the good person test to help start the conversation and get it going in the direction you want it to go, then I'm all for it.

You must have an idea of where you want to take the conversation. Without a clear direction, it's easy to be led on rabbit trails and forget what you wanted to tell them. Having a general plan also helps you to focus and guide the conversation. Certainly, there is no set formula. Each person's needs will be different, but for example, a basic plan for conversation might look like this:

1. Assess spiritual need
2. Address stumbling blocks
3. Use the law
4. Look for signs of repentance
5. Share the gospel

You may only get through a couple of these, and not have the opportunity to share the gospel with every person, but obviously, sharing the gospel is our goal, so be sure to offer to leave tracts with them, even if they end the conversation.

Door to door

Some say that door to door evangelism doesn't work anymore, because they believe that people are not open to it. They suggest that people are too afraid to open their doors and offended by the presence of some stranger at their door. My guess is that the people that say such things have probably never gone door to door; because that certainly has *not* been my experience.

While not everyone is receptive to spiritual conversation at the door, almost all are willing to take a tract or other form of literature. Very few people refuse to take anything; and even fewer still are rude or offended that we came.

The spiritual benefits for those who receive either tracts or a full-blown conversation, including the gospel message, far outweigh the momentary rejection of the few. I can't even count the number of times people have sincerely thanked us for coming to share the gospel with them.

Many people that are completely comfortable bringing up spiritual conversation in other situations shy away from door to door evangelism. Because this type of soul-winning seems to be the most intimidating, I'd like to present most conversations from this perspective, although the principles illustrated are applicable to almost any evangelism.

I'll be honest, I have had moments of gripping fear when I knocked on a door, and I have even hoped that no one was home; but getting past this fear of men is such an enormously freeing blessing.

I knocked, now what?

Many people like to make small talk, complimenting gardens or lawns to start with, which is great; but too much of this can easily eat up time that neither of you have. I'm not good at making small talk, and it's ok if you're not either. If you happen to be going to someone's door, you can bet they want to know why you're there, in a hurry. So, just go ahead and tell them. The direct approach is generally better.

I usually start by introducing myself, telling them what church I'm from and that I'm out passing out tracts and talking to people about the Lord. Telling them what church you attend generally eases their minds by letting them know that you are not a Jehovah's Witness or Mormon. It's also easy to then address their beliefs.

"Do you have a church that you go to?"
"Did you attend at one time, but no longer?"
"Why did you stop?"
"Do you have a Christian background?"

This can *help* to assess their spiritual needs and identify possible stumbling blocks, such as denominational error, sin, or intellectualism. If they claim to believe in God, but have simply lost interest in church you might ask:

"What, in your opinion, is keeping you from having a closer relationship with God"

This question is one that can help even an unsaved, unchurched person identify the stumbling block in their own life. They may immediately express sorrow for having wandered away and be open to the message of reconciliation to God.

Or, they may genuinely consider the question and confess the issue. Often, these things are some form of idolatry, covetousness, immorality, or addiction that generally point to a lack of genuine repentance.

I remember, prior to my salvation, thinking that I wanted to get my life in order, and everything lined up the way I wanted before I looked to God. This was because I was pursuing things in a way that I knew he would not approve of. These sinful pursuits were the things that were keeping me from seeking God, even though I was under conviction.

If they are willing to speak about that which genuinely possesses their hearts, it can help open the conversation toward God's desire for that place in their heart. Using biblical terminology to address these issues can also help to show them the seriousness of them, without feeling like you are throwing stones. You might say, *"the Bible calls that idolatry"* or *"the Bible refers to sexual relationships outside of marriage as fornication."*

Remember, until they see that they are sinners before God, they cannot be saved. They will not embrace the Physician until they recognize their disease. So, don't rush to soothe their conscience. Allow them time to sense the danger of God's wrath.

Other doors you knock on may be answered by those who currently participate in or associate themselves with some sort of religion. They may claim to be Catholic, Methodist, Lutheran…etc. If you do not have a clear understanding of their denominational beliefs to draw from, keep in mind that all other forms of Christianity apart from genuine Bible-believing Christianity (as well as most other false religions) teach a works-based salvation. You could ask, *"What does your church teach that you need to do to get into Heaven?"* This will give you the best sense of what they are really trusting in. Then show them what the Bible teaches about salvation.

You should always plan to have a tract with you that *clearly* spells out the difference between a works-based salvation and salvation by grace through faith. You might use the tract as a teaching source right there and go through it with them. Or you can leave it for them to read later.

Ephesians 2:8-9 were the verses God used to show me the truth of salvation by grace through faith.

"For **by grace are ye saved through faith; and that not of yourselves: it is the gift of God: Not of works,** lest any man should boast." (Ephesians 2:8-9)

Being a former Catholic, I believe I can relate well to those who claim to be Catholic now. Catholics are a proud bunch because they have been taught, as I was, that there is no salvation outside of the Catholic Church. Even those who no longer practice Catholicism still consider themselves part of that elite group.

Because of this, I often tell them that I was raised Catholic and that I am grateful to have learned through that, to believe in God and that Jesus Christ was the sinless Son of God who died for our sins, was buried and rose again.

But... I tell them, there was always one question that troubled me about what we believed. If we can, as we are taught, confess our sins to the priest and do penance, good deeds, or perform the sacraments of the church to atone for our sins; why then did Christ suffer such an extreme, torturous death? It seemed to me that God was unnecessarily harsh toward him if all those other things worked too. Wouldn't it seem that Christ died in vain if there were other ways?

Often, they will confess that it does not make sense. This is the perfect opportunity to discuss in detail, salvation by grace through faith. Verses such as the one below can have a profound influence at this point.

> "I do not frustrate the grace of God: for **if righteousness come by the law, then Christ is dead in vain.**" (Galatians 2:21)

Dealing with those who claim to be saved already (but do not evidence it).

This was a huge roadblock for me in the beginning of my evangelism efforts. I just did not know what to say if they claimed to have already *accepted Jesus* or *asked him into their heart*. After much prayer and much study, I find that the easiest way to address it is to simply ask for their testimony.

I usually say something like, "that's great. I love to hear

people's testimonies. Can I ask how you came to faith in Christ? Was there a particular verse that helped you to understand the gospel?"

Find out what it is they are trusting in. Often, they will reference coming to church as a child, with no testimony of coming to the truth of salvation. Others will appeal to a herd mentality and list all the family members who also attend church as well as the churches they have attended.

If there is no testimony of repentance toward God and genuine faith in Christ, but only a testimony of attending church, or saying a prayer, ask more questions. Many have had a church experience, but not a genuine conversion.

"How did your life change when you got saved?"

"What was it, that God used to show you that you were a sinner on your way to hell at such a young age?"

"The Bible tells us that we are born again by the Indwelling Holy Spirit when we get saved, and that the Holy Spirit will witness of itself. What were the first evidences you recognized of being born again?"

"What is it that makes you sure you are saved?"

These questions will be very difficult for the unsaved. If they seem to struggle, it's probably an indication that they don't really understand salvation or are not saved. If that is the case, take the opportunity to explain man's lost condition and need for rebirth, and evangelize them as you would a lost person.

Others may just be confused by these questions and shut down the conversation. That's ok. The Lord may be simply using you to show them that they are not saved, and to plant a seed today. They must be *lost* before they can be saved.

Before I was genuinely saved, I had been led through a Sinner's Prayer and told that I was saved. (I wasn't.) There was a man that I waited on at work once that spoke of his wife as a born-again Christian. I eagerly offered that I was a Christian as well.

He chuckled, and said, "No. I mean, my wife is a *real*

Christian. She wouldn't even step foot in a place like this."

While that stung quite a bit, God used it to show me that I certainly wasn't living like a Christian. I'm thankful that I eventually came to the truth of my lost condition and was saved.

I have a tract called *Biblical Evidences of Salvation* that I usually leave with those who profess to be saved. It goes through the evidences of the Holy Spirit listed in the Book of 1 John, hopefully exposing the shallowness of a false testimony and lack of biblical evidences in their lives.

If you don't have any literature dealing with the evidences of the Holy Spirit, simply point them to the book of 1 John. Or download a free copy from my website reclaimingbiblicalchristianity.com.

I explain that since I obviously don't know them, I have no way of knowing whether they are saved or not, but that the Bible warns of those who will one day stand before the Lord, believing themselves to be saved. These however will be told, "depart from me, I never knew you." (Matthew 7:23) That is why the Bible tells us to examine ourselves to be sure we are in the faith. It would be terrible for someone to think they are on their way to heaven and instead end up in Hell.

I encourage them to seriously consider their eternal destination and leave information about true salvation as well.

Please resist the urge to give your own assurance of their salvation, but instead point them to the evidences of the Holy Spirit shown in God's word.

> "Hereby know we that we dwell in him, and he in us, because he hath given us of his Spirit." (1 John 4:13)

Good people

Many people we meet are just hoping to get to heaven because they believe they are being good. This is where the application of the law is important.

I usually explain that when we look around at other people, we often seem to be more righteous than them; but that is not the standard that God will use to judge our righteousness. His standard is perfection, represented in his laws. Then I ask if they are familiar with the Ten Commandments. (It is surprising to me how many are not.) Then I ask if we can go through a couple to see how they will do when they stand before God.

> *"Have you ever lied?"*
> *"Have you ever stolen anything?"*
> *"Have you ever taken the Lord's name in vain?"*

By God's unchanging standard, they quickly see that they are not as righteous as they thought. Pointing out the seriousness of even one sin, helps to show them their condemnation before God.

> "For whosoever shall keep the whole law, and yet offend in one point, he is guilty of all." (James 2:10)

> "But the fearful, and unbelieving, and the abominable, and murderers, and whoremongers, and sorcerers, and idolaters, and all liars, shall have their part in the lake which burneth with fire and brimstone: which is the second death."(Revelation 21:8)

Once they see that their condemnation is just and that their hope can only be in a Savior, the gospel begins to make more sense.

A changing generation

In the past, most people you met while soul winning were either members of false religions or false converts. That is quickly changing. This current Millennial generation seems to have a great number of Atheists and Agnostics. The trend toward Bible criticism and access to worldly wisdom has led most away from faith in God.

I recently spoke with a very intelligent young man who, like most today, does not completely deny the existence of God, but expressed his doubts. This young man's reluctance to believe hinged on the age-old question of; *if there is a God, why would he allow things like child abuse, cancer, rape and murder?* The thought behind what he is saying, is *I think God is unloving and unfair, and therefore, not worthy of my worship.*

While I could have sought to prove God's existence and authority to him, I chose to address the underlying issue instead. I asked him if he was a rapist or a murderer; and of course he said he was not. He claimed that he would never do those things; which brought us to the issue of choice. I pointed out that he has the freedom to choose to be kind, considerate and morally upright, while others who have the same freedom can choose to abuse and kill.

God has given us a free will. Although he has provided us with wisdom and guidelines for healthy, happy living, most choose to reject these. Instead we choose to lie, covet, steal, murder, destroy our marriages through adultery, drink and do drugs, and ultimately reject the God who created us.

Even cancer and many other diseases are the result of choices, not always the choice of the victim, but often of chemical and pharmaceutical companies, animal products containing growth hormones, or genetically modified food as well as many other products and services *we* have chosen to produce in spite of the negative effects on our health.

We *now* know that genetically modified foods are not good for us and cause many diseases. God has *always* known this. God's word even warns us against mingling seed.

"Ye shall keep my statutes. Thou shalt not let

thy cattle gender with a diverse kind: **thou shalt not sow thy field with mingled seed:** neither shall a garment mingled of linen and woollen come upon thee." (Leviticus 19:19)

We are free to cultivate the evil desires we have, and reap the consequences, or to submit to God's plan. All of this comes down to the issue of choice and human greed. God's word provides everything we need to guard against such potentially harmful choices at another's expense.

Because we have a choice, we have sin, disease, murder, abuse, rape and every terrible thing there is. What is the alternative? The only way to prevent sin and disease in the world would be to remove our ability to choose. If you remember, Adam and Eve lived in perfection, yet because of their free will, they brought sin and death into the world.

God could have simply made us without a will of our own and forced us to obey and live the way he says is best; but then we would accuse him of unfairness because of *that*.

The young man I spoke with agreed that it would seem even more unfair if we were simply robots without a will of our own. He did not get saved that day, but possibly gained another perspective of God.

It is not God's choice that sin and sickness happen to the extent that they do today. It's ours. God offers a better way, but man chooses to reject it.

Avoiding rabbit trails.

Some people like this young man, have sincere questions and need to be patiently instructed, answering their concerns according to Scripture, and helping to remove stumbling blocks. Others have no interest in spiritual things.

It's important to be able to recognize the difference. Scorners and skeptics will gladly waste your time with a feigned interest in God, while attempting to disprove him to you and any others within earshot.

Atheists will often engage you intellectually, taking you on every rabbit trail imaginable and asking every illogical, and irrelevant question they can come up with simply as an attempt to confuse you. According to the Bible, Atheists are fools, whose only desire is to promote their foolishness. This is what God has to say about dealing with fools:

> "Speak not in the ears of a fool: for he will despise the wisdom of thy words" (Proverbs 23:9).

They may even flatter you with a false interest in your Bible knowledge. This is most often meant to mock you, not to learn from you. It's important to understand this.

> "But foolish and unlearned questions avoid, knowing that they do gender strifes." (2 Timothy 2:23)

Sometimes, these questions are not sincere and even answering them will not lead to their enlightenment or belief, but simply to more questions. If they can stump you with their questions, they have in their own minds justified their unbelief.

> "A fool hath no delight in understanding, but that his heart may discover itself." (Proverbs 18:2)

This may seem harsh and unloving, but God knows far better than we do how they should be handled. He knows that it is a great waste of time to argue with a fool; because it is *not a lack of knowledge* that causes unbelief, but the *willful rejection* of the knowledge of God.

> "The heavens declare the glory of God; and the firmament sheweth his handywork. Day unto day uttereth speech, and night unto night sheweth knowledge. There is no speech nor language, where their

voice is not heard" (Psalms 19:1).

God has not called us to prove his existence to Atheists or to anyone else. He has already done that.

"Because that which may be known of God is manifest in them; for God hath shewed it unto them. For the invisible things of him from the creation of the world are clearly seen, being understood by the things that are made, even his eternal power and Godhead; so that they are without excuse: Because that, when they knew God, they glorified him not as God, neither were thankful; but became vain in their imaginations, and their foolish heart was darkened. Professing themselves to be wise, they became fools" (Romans 1:19-22).

The reason they reject the knowledge of God is simple. They do not want to submit to his authority. God has called us to share the gospel- the reason for the hope that is within us. We are to be making disciples through spreading the gospel. If they will not believe in God, then they cannot receive the gospel and be reconciled to him.

"But without faith it is impossible to please him: for he that cometh to God must believe that he is, and that he is a rewarder of them that diligently seek him" (Hebrews 11:6).

I know that many today believe that apologetics is the answer. While apologetics certainly has its place; it is often *only* to remove intellectual stumbling-blocks and to educate believers. You could choose to argue apologetics all day long, disproving their illogical philosophies; but you cannot argue anyone into Heaven.

Every person you meet has a different philosophy and standard of morality; but the one thing they all have in common is a conscience. If you do not find a way to address the conscience, it is merely a war of words. Remember, it is the law that is *perfect, converting the soul*, not philosophy.

We need to be obedient to God's word and not lean to our own understanding. When they will not believe in God, we must brush the dust off our feet and keep going. We cannot allow them to keep us from our commission. There are some out there with repentant hearts ready to receive the good news!

Many times, we want so badly for people to see the truth that we chase these rabbit trails far beyond what is profitable. As a matter of fact, most often we do more harm than good when we engage them. Doing this in front of others can become even more disastrous.

Do's

Do be prayed up and Spirit-led- Prayer is powerful! Trust the Lord to lead you by his Spirit. Yielding to him is far better than holding to any plan of your own. If you know and read your Bible, he *will* bring to your mind the verses and the words you need *when* you need them.

Do try (as far as you are able) **to assess the spiritual condition-** Look for evidences of conviction and repentance. Remember, someone who is blinded by their sin, whose heart is far from God cannot sense his need for a Savior. Offering Jesus to someone like this is only foolishness to them. It is doubtful (but not impossible!) that you will see a quick conversion; but there may be a great opportunity to help develop a fear of the Lord and encourage repentance.

You may be called today to be a John the Baptist and help prepare their heart for the Savior. At the very least warn them of their imminent danger as much as the conversation will allow.

"… pulling them out of the fire; hating even the

garment spotted by the flesh." (Jude 1:23)

Do leave biblical information- It is the word that saves, so try to give them as much of it as they will take. I always try to have a free Bible to offer, John and Romans booklets, discipleship booklets for new Christians, as well as tracts. I can't stress how much I would caution against giving tracts with a Sinner's Prayer. This can lead the lost to think they are saved because they prayed, when they are not.

It's important to have a variety of tracts, some specific to Catholics, some simply dealing with the works-based salvation issue, …etc. Having one with a strong message of repentance and reconciliation to God is essential. I also like to carry some on the biblical evidences of salvation/being born again, and a good person test …etc.

Many of these tracts, I have written myself, to address specific situations I've encountered, like one entitled *Won't God Just Forgive My Sins?* for those who believe they will simply ask God for forgiveness when they get to Heaven. This is a surprisingly common response.

There are many tract printing ministries that offer free tracts. It can be difficult to find tracts without a Sinner's Prayer. If you cannot find what you are looking for, I offer free printable tracts on my website: reclaimingbiblicalchristianity.com. These are each formatted as a Pdf and can be downloaded as a tri-fold two-sided tract for 8 ½ by 11inch paper. The larger brochure size often piques the interest. I like to print them on bright colored paper for festivals and parades.

Do use the law- It is the law that shows God's holiness in comparison to our own sinfulness and brings us to the understanding of his just judgement upon us. Until they see their true condition *as a sinner condemned* to hell, they will not embrace *Jesus as their Savior.*

"The law of the LORD is perfect, converting the

soul: the testimony of the LORD is sure, making wise the simple." (Psalms 19:7)

Do call sinners to repent and be reconciled to God- It is vitally important to keep in mind that we are not sent to beg people to accept Jesus, as though they are doing him a favor, or to offer them a free ticket to heaven. We are sent with the message of reconciliation to our great and holy God, and this can only happen through repentance toward him and faith toward Christ.

If we are too afraid to call sinners to repentance, then we are too afraid to share the gospel message.

"I came not to call the righteous, but sinners to repentance." (Luke 5:32)

Don'ts

Don't use unbiblical catch phrases- such as *ask Jesus into your heart* or *accept Jesus*. Even the biblical terms *saved*, *born-again*, and *salvation* can be confusing and may need to be defined. Repentance is another word that may need clarification because of its lack of use and misuse.

Don't use leading questions- such as *are you saved?* Or *has there been a time in your life that...?* The answer to these is always yes. After that, there is almost nowhere to go. Ask questions that demand answers, not *yes or no* questions.

Don't rush a decision- While we want to persuade sinners to repent and trust Christ, we must also allow the Holy Spirit to do his job. It is not our job to lead them through a prayer or pronounce them saved. No matter how strongly we desire to convince them to turn to God, we should never seem like fast-talking salesmen with gimmicks and trickery. We are merely faithful messengers sent to lovingly plead with the lost.

Don't give a false assurance- We are called to preach the gospel, baptize believers, and to disciple them. If someone claims to believe, remember to offer only biblical instructions. It is not our job to seal the deal with a prayer or any assurance of our own. We are to instruct those who believe to be baptized and to join themselves to a local Bible-believing church to learn, grow, and serve.

Don't take it personally- If they reject your efforts. They aren't rejecting us, but God. Be gracious even in rejection. Leave them open to receive from future Christians.

Don't get discouraged- It takes time to learn how to share the gospel effectively. I was a silent partner for years before I felt comfortable doing it. Don't feel pressured, go with someone else that is experienced until you are ready. The resources below may help you to build confidence.

Resources

The Way of the Master training course
https://www.livingwaters.com

Will Our Generation Speak? by Grace Malley- Tremendously encouraging book about evangelizing.
https://www.amazon.com/Will-Our-Generation-Speak-Gospel/dp/0971940584

Preach-o-matic Portable preaching display, simple design requires much less time and energy to set up than a booth.
www.oacusaold.com/preachomatic/home.htm

Amazing Grace ministries Information and instruction for marketplace evangelism. Fair and festival booths.

www.agm-ffci.org/home.asp

Fellowship tract league Free tracts
fellowshiptractleague.org

Liberty Bible Courses Free gospel tracts and discipleship booklets, in several languages.
www.libertygospeltracts.com/Biblecrs/Biblecrs.htm

CONCLUSION

Are we glorifying God?

When I began writing this book, it was primarily to disprove the modern Sinner's Prayer method of evangelism; and to promote a more biblical evangelism that would lead more souls to Christ.

It wasn't long into my studies, before God showed me that even those motives *could not* be the priority. *He* is the priority. *Glorifying him* in all that we say and do *is* the priority.

Although I was well-aware of the history of God's chosen people and their rejection of him; seeing God's heart and his tender mercies toward them broke my heart *for Him* anew. I was convicted of so many of the same attitudes and failures toward him.

Seeing God's command, *Behold me, behold me*, gave me a whole new sense of the seriousness of what we as Christians are called to do. My desire now is not to merely *get people saved*, but to show God's greatness and power to all the world, so that they will behold him and glorify him the way he deserves.

I hope that through reading this book, you have seen him through new eyes as well, and have that same desire. It can be easy to think we are glorifying God when we are involved with ministries in the church. Busyness is often mistaken for spirituality as we become consumed with the details of our ministries and traditions, losing sight of *why* we do what we do.

Even sincere, godly ministries can lose their sweet-smelling savor to God if we aren't seeking his glory first. When was the last time you truly stopped to simply behold our great and glorious God?

We can share *a gospel message* with every person we meet,

but if we are not sharing the true gospel, calling them to be reconciled to our holy God, leading them to a restored relationship with *him*, we are *not* glorifying God.

Today's modern gospel is not only flawed doctrinally, but in its focus as well. It is *man-centered* rather than *God-centered*, inviting the lost to partake of the *benefits* of salvation: love, joy, peace and eternal life, rather than reconciliation with God.

While I frequently hear soul winners describe salvation as *a relationship and not a religion,* the nature of that relationship is often skewed. Our relationship with God *prior to salvation* can only be that of a helplessly lost sinner on our way to hell, unable to do anything at all to save ourselves. Our only hope is to humble ourselves, falling on our faces before our creator and seeking his mercy. That is when our loving Father extends his hand of mercy toward us and gives to us what we do not deserve: salvation and forgiveness of sins through Jesus Christ.

After salvation, our relationship should be one of awe and worship and eternal gratitude. We are saved, *not* for our own pleasure or purpose, but *to glorify God!* We are created to be used for his purposes, not just to escape hell and receive blessings. A relationship based on a reluctant acceptance of Jesus for the purpose of escaping hell is not the relationship described in God's word!

Are we leading others to behold our great and holy God, or are we merely encouraging lip-service? No matter how sincere we may be, if the gospel we are preaching is not the true gospel message, we are *not* glorifying God and everything we are doing is for nothing. If we are honoring him with our lips while our hearts are far from him, or leading others to think they can come to him this way, we are no better than the idolatrous Jews.

ABOUT
THE AUTHOR

Author of *Seasons of Life: Man's Journey from the Garden to Glory*, *Why Are We Losing the Kids?* and *The Beginning of Wisdom: God's Plan for Bringing Children to Faith,* S. M Platt, a former false convert, has a passion for God's word and a strong desire to see souls come to a genuine knowledge of salvation.

Available on Amazon

References

Craven, S. Michael. "Fathers: Key to Their Children's Faith." The Christian Post, The Christian Post, 19 June 2011, https://www.christianpost.com/news/fathers-key-to-their-childrens-faith.html.KJV

Genesis 4 Benson Commentary, https://Biblehub.com/commentaries/benson/genesis/4.htm.

House, Polly. "Want Your Church to Grow? Then Bring in the Men." Baptist Press, 3 Apr. 2003, http://www.bpnews.net/15630.

Jamieson, Fausset & Brown,. "Commentary on Exodus 30 by Jamieson, Fausset & Brown." Blue Letter Bible. Last modified 19 Feb, 2000. http://www.blueletterBible.org/Comm/jfb/Exd/Exd_030.cfm

Ross, Thomas. "The Sinners Prayer: A Historical and Theological Analysis." Faith Saves, 17 June 2017, https://faithsaves.net/the-sinners-prayer/.

"G868 - aphistēmi - Strong's Greek Lexicon (KJV)." Blue Letter Bible. Web. 28 Sep, 2019. <https://www.blueletterBible.org//lang/Lexicon/Lexicon.cfm?Strongs=G868&t=KJV>.

"G1519 - eis - Strong's Greek Lexicon (KJV)." Blue Letter Bible. Web. 28 Sep, 2019.
<https://www.blueletterBible.org//lang/Lexicon/Lexicon.cfm?Strongs=G1519&t=KJV>.

"G1941 - epikaleō - Strong's Greek Lexicon (KJV)." Blue Letter Bible. Web. 28 Sep, 2019.
<https://www.blueletterBible.org//lang/lexicon/lexicon.cfm?Strongs=G1941&t=KJV>.

"G3670 - homologeō - Strong's Greek Lexicon (KJV)." Blue Letter Bible. Web. 28 Sep, 2019.
<https://www.blueletterBible.org//lang/Lexicon/Lexicon.cfm?Strongs=G3670&t=KJV>.

"G4624 - skandalizō - Strong's Greek Lexicon (KJV)." Blue Letter Bible. Web. 28 Sep, 2019.
<https://www.blueletterBible.org//lang/Lexicon/Lexicon.cfm?Strongs=G4624&t=KJV>.

Made in the USA
Coppell, TX
17 November 2024